Leadership Mentality

Twenty
Common Sense
Chapters on Leadership

Dr. Neal Weaver

Eagle Publications
Shreveport, Louisiana

Leadership Mentality

Revised Edition Printed in 2018

ISBN: 0692165452

ISBN 13: 9780692165454

All Scripture quotations are taken from the King James Version of the Bible.

Editing: Book Creators for Pastors; Kit R. Olsen, MA.

Published by Eagle Publications
Shreveport, Louisiana

Printed in the United States of America.

"But they that wait upon the LORD shall renew [their] strength; they shall mount up with wings as eagles; they shall run, and not be weary; [and] they shall walk, and not faint."

—Isaiah 40:31

This book is dedicated to my daughter Kim and my son Scott—two of the greatest supporters a dad could ever hope to have; and to all those who have assisted in my life's journey. My thanks to Peggy Magill who typed the original manuscript. Special thanks to Kit R. Olsen who spent countless hours editing and preparing the manuscript for final publication.

Success is…
Knowing your purpose in life.
Growing to reach your maximum potential.
And sowing seeds that benefit others.

—John C. Maxwell

Contents

Preface

This book is a composite of insights I have gained throughout fifty-seven years of experience as a pastor and educator. Hopefully these insights will give you an advantage I did not have, and keep you from having to learn some of the lessons I had to learn. In every field, whether it is secular or religious, there is a demand for leadership. In business and industry, dynamic leadership is much sought after and is well-compensated.

Today's increasing demands on our church and ministry leaders necessitates the ongoing development of outstanding leaders. Developing effective leaders is an essential requirement for the continued growth of any ministry. Leadership is a key ingredient to success, whether it is in the pulpit, classroom or a corporate office. Virtually everyone will lead in some capacity or another, either professionally or as a leader in the home.

"Inexperienced leaders are quick to lead before knowing anything about the people they intend to lead. But mature leaders listen, learn and then lead."

—John Maxwell

Chapter One

Leaders Develop by Using A Positive Attitude

Finally, brethren, whatsoever things are true, whatsoever things are honest, whatsoever things are just, whatsoever things are pure, whatsoever things are lovely, whatsoever things are of good report; if there be any virtue, and if there be any praise, think on these things. — Philippians 4:8

Every success, regardless of its nature begins with a positive state of mind. A positive mental attitude is the starting point of all personal achievements, material or spiritual. I have heard of many people who were fortunate enough to be born into fame or fortune. But I have never heard of a single soul who became a successful leader by accident. Successful leaders begin with a positive attitude, and through hard work, sacrifices and perseverance—accomplish the success they envision. It may take years of dedication, but it all begins with an unwavering positive attitude.

Dr. Earl Williams in his book titled, *Golden Keys* states, "It is highly significant that the Creator provided man with control over nothing except the power to shape his own destiny by and through rational thought." The attitude of the mind shapes all aspects of our lives, even our physical well-being. One of the most extraordinary stories I have ever heard is that of a wandering hobo. It seems that one night he was accidentally locked inside a refrigerated rail car.

The lock malfunctioned and the hobo could not open the door. Somewhere inside the rail car he found a piece of chalk and throughout the night he chronicled what took place as he slowly froze to death. In the morning he was found dead. All this took place in spite of the fact that the refrigerated car was disconnected and never fell beneath 45 degrees. In his mind he was freezing to death and his body acted accordingly.

It is a proven fact that a positive mental attitude can be a very important factor in both the physical well-being and the healing processes of the body. Not only must we develop a positive mental attitude, but we must also develop a positive plan of action for our lives. In over fifty years as pastor, evangelist, radio executive and educator, I have observed the sad fact that many people who are involved in Christian service, more often than not—maintain a self-defeating philosophy of negativity. Their emphasis is always on what Christians should give up, not on what they should accomplish. Christians should make every effort to do all they can to rid themselves of blatant sins, and unproductive habits that hinder their testimony, damage their character and minimize their ability to serve the Lord.

However, it is not just a case of quitting drunkenness, adultery, dishonesty or other sins; our responsibility is also a matter of dealing with things that hinder us from being all we should be for God. The apostle Paul said, "All things are lawful for me, but all things are not expedient." Being a good Christian is more than just being a good "quitter." A Christian's life should be a life of accomplishments, satisfaction and positive actions. It is not enough that a child of God has given up a decadent lifestyle. Saved individuals should also be actively involved in excellent endeavors that not only improve their lot in life, but also serve as a good witness to those around them—to those who serve God earnestly and exuberantly.

James 4:17 says, "Therefore to him that knoweth to do good, and doeth it not, to him it is sin." Many people are fairly good quitters of sinful habits but are chronic sinners when it comes to the sin of omission. They have not pursued the positive things that honor God to make their own lives truly successful. For example, Christians should never be slothful in their work, dishonest in their dealings, wasteful of the time God has given them or negative in their thinking. Their traits should be positive and with purpose. Hard work, honesty, the proper use of time and a positive attitude will ultimately bring success both personally and with God. There are three types of Christians in the world:

- Those who "make things happen."
- Those who "watch things happen."
- Those who say, "what happened?"

This was true even in Jesus' day. The apostle Peter was always asking our Lord "Why?" He was always getting into trouble. He was always talking when he should have been quiet and listening. He even denied the Lord three times. But Peter was definitely a "make things happen" Christian. He became one of the most powerful leaders of the early church. I cannot write about the "make things happen" Christian without writing about the apostle Paul. He did more to make things happen than any other person since the Lord Jesus ascended into heaven. He was beaten, stoned and put in prison. But that did not stop him from making things happen for the Lord. Both Peter and Paul were killed because of their witness for the Lord Jesus. They were both "make things happen" Christians.

Jesus appointed twelve chosen disciples to be His close followers. We all know about Peter, James, John, Matthew and perhaps Thomas. But what about the others? We know that Peter was a "make things happen" man. James was one of the first Christian martyrs; John was exiled to the Isle of Patmos for his witness, and Thomas is known for being the doubter. We know that Judas betrayed the Lord Jesus and then hanged himself. But what about the others? Very little is said about them in the Scriptures. Would you agree that they could fall into the "watch things happen" group? They did what they were told, they didn't make trouble, they didn't draw attention to the group—they were JUST THERE. They "watched things happen" around them.

We are all familiar with the Twelve Disciples of Jesus, but did you know that He appointed seventy more and sent them out? We read in the Gospel of Luke (10:1-7) that Jesus appointed seventy more disciples; that the seventy returned with joy and said that even the devils are subject to them in His name. But what about after that? What became of those men? They did what they were told to do, when they were told to do it—but they didn't pursue anything on their own to further the cause of Christ. No mention of those seventy disciples is made again anywhere in the Bible; only in that one chapter in the book of Luke. Would not you agree that they were "what happened?" Christians?

- Are you a "make things happen" Christian?
- Are you a "watch things happen" Christian?
- Or are you a "what happened" Christian?

Do you look for things that need to be done and do them without being asked? Do you send a card or note to sick, grieving, lonely or troubled souls? Do you make it a point to invite someone to church with you each week? Do you ask the pastor, teachers or others if they need help? Do you pray daily for your pastor, deacons, elders and teachers?

Or...do you show up at church once a month and complain because, "The pastor preached too long again today." Do you avoid talking about church because you don't want to offend anyone? Do you watch the late night news and then you're too tired to pray?

Or...do you show up on Christmas and Easter and complain about the hypocrites who go to church every week? Do you complain that all the preacher wants is money?

Where do you fit in? Are you a Christian who wants to make things happen for Jesus? Are you satisfied with watching others make things happen for Jesus? Will you stand before Him someday and say, "Wow man, what happened?" True success is built around your relationship with God, your relationship with others, how you feel about yourself and a proven value system. Many people have placed their careers at the top of their priority lists, and have succeeded in becoming quite wealthy—but they are miserable. During their climb to the top and rise to prosperity they neglected their fellowship with God, neglected their responsibilities to their families, and compromised their values. Then after accomplishing all their goals, they find that they are unhappy and their lives are not fulfilling.

This book deals with the promise of how we can take positive actions as well as keep other aspects of our lives in balance. It will give direction on how true leadership involves commitment, hard work, organization, good personal habits, dedication to those we love, and most of all—our undeniable and necessary dependence on God. All riches—of whatever nature, begin as a state-of-mind. And let us remember that a state of mind is the one and only thing over which any person has the complete right to control.

Dr. Williams' analysis is right when he said, "It is highly significant that the Creator provided mankind with control over nothing except the power to shape his own destiny by and through rational thought." A positive mental attitude is the starting point of all personal achievements, whether it be in the material or spiritual realm. It attracts the riches of true friendships and the riches one finds in the hope of future achievements.

While I would be one of the first to point out that certain writers and speakers have taken positive thinking to a point where they leave God out of their messages, I believe that the positive-minded person under God's direction can accomplish amazing things. Developing a positive mental attitude is an important step we must take, in the control and direction of our minds. This is a necessary principle because all degrees of a negative mental attitude leave us wide open to every adverse influence that may come our way.

A positive mental attitude is the only condition of the mind that we can gain the wisdom with which to recognize the true purpose of life, and adapt ourselves to that purpose. A positive mental attitude is a "must" for all who make life what it should be and can be. In his book, *Golden Keys*, Dr. Earl Williams makes these outstanding, thought-provoking points:

Five Excellent Steps One Can Take to Develop a Positive Mental Attitude

1. You can recognize your privilege of taking possession of and using your own mind, as being the one and only thing over which you have complete control.

2. You can recognize and prove to your own satisfaction the truth that every adversity carries with it the seed of an equivalent bene it.

3. You can learn to close the door behind you on all failures and unpleasant circumstances you may have experienced in the past.

4. You can begin to put into action a powerful success principle: The habit of going the extra mile.

5. You can select a pacemaker (role model) and emulate him or her in every possible way.

People who have a positive mental outlook have confidence in God and the abilities He has given them. They reach decisions promptly and definitely know what they want, and also usually get it. Leaders must make decisions quickly and firmly; that is why they are leaders. Sometimes we hear someone referred to as a "natural born leader." Occasionally, that may be true. But more often than not, leaders are people who started out in obscure circumstances and through a positive attitude, fortitude and persistence—rose to prominent positions.

I remember quite clearly while in my junior year in high school I promised myself I would not drift through life; I wanted to be a leader. I do not know why I made that declaration. I was not especially gifted at anything and preferred to stand back and let others lead. I think that is still my true nature. But with God's help and a positive determination, I have been able to do far more than I ever had a right to expect. Being a shy backwoods boy who had never given a public speech, I certainly never expected the Lord to call me into Christian ministry. Yet He has let me speak in some of the greatest churches in America, and to thousands of people in foreign countries. We are admonished that what we accomplish is not by our might or power but by the power of Almighty God.

I had the privilege of being acquainted with the late great evangelist, Lester Rolloff. I spoke to him on the phone the day before he died in a tragic plane crash. He was scheduled to speak as my guest at an event the day after his accident. On the evening of the meeting where Dr. Rolloff was to speak, we instead held a tribute to his ministry. A few days just before his death, he had sent me a special gift. It was a beautifully varnished wood plaque and on it was carved this verse:

> "For God hath not given us the spirit of fear; but of power, and of love, and of a sound mind" (2 Timothy 1:7).

I have gone to that verse so many times when my confidence failed and the obstacles seemed too great to overcome. I believe it is scriptural and right for us to have a positive confidence that we can accomplish great things—especially great things for God. You may ask, "What about humility?" Humility is recognizing that everything that we accomplish is through God.

I remember an old hound dog my family had on our farm when I was a boy. If one person spoke a stern word or another dog growled at him, that hound would hump his back, tuck his tail and slink off to the barn to hide. According to some people, by their definition, he would have been the world's most humble dog. I believe there is nothing prideful or unscriptural about rising up and saying, "I want to accomplish all I can within the parameters of God's will."

Jesus expects fruit, not excuses for not bearing fruit. The barren fig tree of Luke 13:6-7 is a good illustration of God's attitude toward a barren fig tree. The fig tree, planted in the orchard to bear fruit utterly failed in the purpose for which it was created. Many Christians unnecessarily fail both personally and spiritually. They do not commit open or vicarious sins; socially and morally their lives are impeccable. The great tragedy is their lives are barren of the real fruit of the Christian life. Each one of us is given different talents. Some will naturally rise higher than others. The important precept for all of us to remember is not to bury our God-given talents and abilities.

It is important that we establish a positive philosophy that says, "I want to accomplish all that God sets before me." Perhaps you have heard this saying, "I am only one person and I cannot accomplish all things but those things that I can accomplish, I shall." This study on becoming a successful leader in life is different from most self-help books currently on the market. It will first of all define success differently than the current trend that measures success only financially and socially. It will point out that true success is finding God's will for your life, and then giving your all to accomplish it (with the talents with which He has blessed you). It will also point out that everything we achieve must come from God; all our talents, abilities and intellect are God-given and all the glory must be given to Him for everything we achieve.

We are to love the Lord completely without reservation. In the book of Matthew, the Lord's response to the lawyer who was trying to tempt Him by asking, "Master, which is the great commandment in the law?" was true then and remains true today:

> "Jesus said unto him, Thou shalt love the Lord thy God with all thy heart, and with all thy soul, and with all thy mind" (Matthew 22:37).

We are to face this journey called life not in fear, but with full confidence of success because we are instilled with His power. A positive mental attitude is the starting point of all personal achievement, whether it be in the material or spiritual realm. You either use your brain for controlled thinking in connection with things you want, or nature steps in and uses your thinking to grow for you a crop of negative thinking, and negative circumstances which you do not want. You have a God-given choice in this connection. You can take possession of your thought power or allow yourself to be influenced by undesirable stray winds of random circumstances.

"For God hath not given us the spirit of fear; but of power, and of love, and of a sound mind" (2 Timothy 1:7).

With a positive mental attitude you can put your mind to work believing in achievement, and that belief will guide you unerringly toward whatever your desired outcome may be. With that same mind operating through a negative mental attitude, you can believe in fear, frustration, failure and your mind will attract to you the fruits of those undesirable things. Just as there are many rewards of positive thinking, there are equally many consequences of negative thinking.

Rewards of a Positive Mental Attitude

- The privilege of placing one's self on the "Success Beam" which attracts only the circumstances which make for successful achievement.
- Sound health, mentally, physically and spiritually.
- Financial strength and independence.
- A labor of love in which to express one's self.
- Peace of mind.
- Applied faith which makes fear impossible.
- Enduring friendships.
- Longevity and a well-balanced life.
- Immunity against self-limitations.
- The wisdom with which to understand yourself and others.

Penalties of a Negative Mental Attitude

- Poverty—Want—Misery.
- Mental and physical ailments of many kinds.
- Self-limitation which binds one to mediocrity.
- Fear in all of its destructive forces.
- Enemies—few friends.
- Every brand of worry.
- A victim of all negative influences which one encounters.
- Subject to the influence and control of other people.
- A wasted life which gives nothing to the betterment of mankind.

A powerful quote that has been expressed by many people over the years still rings true today: "There is nothing more powerful than the made-up mind." The apostle Paul in his letter to the Corinthians wrote:

> "I am determined to know nothing among you except Christ and Him crucified" (1 Corinthians 2:2).

This definitive statement made by the apostle Paul—to let no one or nothing deter him from his purpose, caused him to become the one, whom most agree, to be heralded as the greatest preacher since Christ's personal ministry.

In Summary

Always remember that this life is not about ourselves—about *our* abilities, *our* talents, *our* intellect or *our* personalities. It is about Christ and what we can accomplish *through* Him. I never cease to be amazed at where He has taken me and all that He has allowed me to do. It simply solidifies the fact that God can take everyday ordinary people and do extraordinary things if we will only let Him use us.

We must seize the day every day. Life is a gift from God to use for His glory.

Chapter Two

Leaders Seize the Day

This is the day which the Lord hath made, we will rejoice and be glad in it.
—Psalm 118:24

We can't always make things great, but we should do everything in our power to make them better. In Ephesians 5:16, we are told to redeem the time because the days are evil. We should look at every day as an opportunity to serve God, serve others and serve ourselves. When we place serving God first, it is then that we have our priorities right. When we place serving others above ourselves then we eliminate selfishness, covetness, envy and jealousy from our lives.

These four characteristics: **selfishness, covetousness, envy** and **jealousy** all cause negativity and are counter-productive to personal success. Many times, while my children were growing up I would hear them say, "That isn't fair." My reply was, "You may be right but who told you life is fair?" I have often prototyped life as a bulldog that sits outside your door. Each day when you go out the door and face the day—you have to face the bulldog. You either whip him or he whips you. We must *seize the day*, every day. We must make it work *for* us instead of *against* us. Do you realize that life itself is a gift to be used for God's glory? Many times I have met people that if you dared ask how things were going, you knew you would always receive a negative answer. Things were always unfavorable. They were always in a dilemma.

All of us have tragedy and conflict in our lives. We all face financial set backs, lose loved ones, lose jobs, etc. It is not a question of *if* we will have to face some of those things, but *when.* When we experience unfavorable circumstances of any kind, we feel all the human emotions: Grief, sense of loss, depression and immobility—causing us to temporarily cease all activity. The question then arises, "How long will this slow me down?" (Notice I said **slow** me down **not stop** me.) Many years ago I heard a speaker say that people can be measured by what it takes to stop them. I decided on that day, as a young man, that it would take a great deal to stop me. I once read a quote somewhere that said, "I cannot control the circumstances that surround me but I can control my attitude within those circumstances."

Perhaps the best advice I ever received goes something like this: Whenever you run into a fence, start looking for the hole. I have passed that advice on many times. In other words, when you hit a fence that seems to stop you, begin to figure out how you can overcome it. Invariably, there is a way to overcome the obstacle and continue to make progress. Those who approach the day with a pessimistic attitude will frequently obtain negative results. Those who face each day as a new challenge and with a positive attitude often emerge as winners. They are the ones who succeed.

I am not preaching instant success and gratification. Many times, achieving your full potential is a long process that may encounter several setbacks. The point is this: Without a positive faith in God and a positive mental attitude, you will not endure through the difficulties and continue toward your goals. Today, most churches are populated with members who are more content with filling a pew than being filled with the Holy Spirit.

In his book, *Design for Living*, J. Dwight Pentecost makes this statement: "Spiritual growth, spiritual development and spiritual health are inseparably united to spiritual appetite." Why is there little or no spiritual appetite so often by so many people? Where is the power that drives men and women to want to succeed? Instead of seizing the day why are so many willing to sit in complacency? I believe that we can isolate at least three common causes: A wrong focus, a wrong friendship, and a wrong fear.

A Wrong Focus

Many Christians have embraced a wrong focus. In what we often refer to as "The Lord's Prayer" (more correctly titled, "The Model Prayer") Christ said to His disciples, "For thine is the kingdom, and the power, and the glory for ever. Amen" (Matthew 6:13b). Instead of correctly focusing on "Thine," many believers wrongly substitute "Mine." Whenever our goals are based on personal benefits instead of the glory of God and the good of others, our lives cannot be in the center of God's will.

A Wrong Friendship

Many Christians possess a wrong friendship. James asked, "Know ye not that the friendship of the world is enmity with God?" (James 4:4). As the hymn, "Am I a Soldier of the Cross?" puts it, "Is this vile world a friend to grace, to help me on to God?" No! This world is corrupt and anti-God. In order to serve our Lord, we must be prepared to separate from the world's philosophies, values and practices. Our citizenship in heaven should be reflected in every area of our lives.

A Wrong Fear

Finally, many Christians today are saddled by a wrong fear. Matthew commands us to "Fear not them which kill the body, but are not able to kill the soul: but rather fear him which is able to destroy both soul and body in hell"(Matthew 10:28). Believers should have a proper fear for the God whom they know and serve. Instead of worrying about the reactions of family members or coworkers, we should leave our actions to the litmus test of Almighty God. Until we are more concerned about God's opinion than anyone else's, we will not be sold-out Christians.

The apostle Paul said, "Hence forth let no man trouble me." He resolved that nothing would deter him from his goal. Many fail to accomplish what they envision because they are content to exchange success for an excuse. In a six-hour workshop in the Bahamas, I used one entire session on the topic of "Eliminating Excuses." Excuses can come from many sources. One excuse I commonly hear is poverty or lack of opportunity. I do not believe either of those circumstances are reasons to fail.

I come from a loving family. I had two great parents. They taught me much about the values of life. I was taught to respect all people, regardless of their race or place in life. I also come from a home that did not have a lot materially. We never wanted for enough to eat or enough love, but we had very little money.

As I completed high school, it was apparent that my parents could not send me to college, but it was never in their plans or mine that I would not attend. As that time approached, I spent the summer working all types of jobs to earn my first semester's tuition. When I enrolled, I worked at various jobs such as delivering newspapers, picking strawberries, cleaning out cow barns, mopping floors in local stores, and cutting grass. I spent a number of years as a full-time student while working a full-time job to feed my family (as well as pastoring a church on weekends).

It was a long seven years as I earned my Bachelors, Masters, and finally Doctorate of Theology degrees. Thankfully, I had a supportive wife and children who understood how thin I was spread. My goal was not easy but it was attainable. The easy way would have been to salve my conscious with the excuse that I would have liked to attend college, but I couldn't afford to go.

Perhaps the most extraordinary story I have ever heard was told to me many years ago by a pastor from Miami. It was about a girl who was paralyzed from the waist down. She had a great burden to find a way to serve God. Each day she would have someone push her wheelchair to a busy street in downtown Miami, and leave her there so she could hand out religious tracts. By the time someone returned to take her home, the metal parts on the wheelchair would be too hot to touch with the naked hand. We can only imagine how many souls were touched by this young lady, who was simply not willing to accept an excuse.

I have always had a great respect for my brother, Carl. When he was three years old he was stricken with polio; so severely that it affected one of his legs. From the very beginning he was a trooper. I have never once heard him voice one word of self-pity. In spite of the fact that he has always had a pronounced limp, and has, for many years walked with a cane—he earned his Master's in Education degree, and for many years held a very respected position in one of the larger high schools in his state.

Carl has always been an avid sports fan. Because of his handicap he was never able to participate in competitive sports, but he studied them. Regardless of his circumstances he became an excellent coach, and over the years he has coached or helped coach several championship baseball teams. Carl has been a contributing force to his community.

Over a period of twenty-five to thirty years, he at sometime has taught almost everyone who attended the large consolidated high school, which serves the entire city and county where he lives. Most places I visit, I am introduced as Dr. Weaver, president of Louisiana Baptist University. When I return to my hometown, London, Kentucky (all too infrequently), I am simply introduced as Carl Weaver's brother; and I am so proud to be introduced in that way.

This next point is very important: Avoid negative people. If you run with a negative thinking crowd you will soon think as they think. In many of my workshops I use the phrase, "Avoid the sour balls." At best, they will make your face take on a scowl and at worst, cause you to abandon a good idea that could have worked.

I am by nature a positive person but I have learned that I must also be surrounded by positive people. In spite of all the messages I have preached on positive thinking, if you put me in too long with a group of doom-mongers—I will begin to think like them. Choose your friends carefully because before long, you will become like them.

No one has ever accomplished much with a negative, depressed attitude. Depression will stop you in your tracks. There is an actual physical condition termed Clinical Depression. This can be a very serious condition requiring professional treatment. Most of us, however, do not suffer from Clinical Depression—just a good dose of self-pity and negative thinking. All of us, at some time in our lives have thrown a first class pity party. Pity parties are always easy to arrange because you are the only guest.

I don't know about you, but I have thrown some dandy pity parties. They lasted for days, even entire weekends. I have sat in semi-darkness while I convinced myself that I was neglected, mistreated, and under-appreciated. We can expend a lot of energy on self-pity, self-recrimination and worry. But it is kind of like rocking in a rocking chair—lots of effort but no forward motion. If we are to seize the day and accomplish what God intends for our lives, we must avoid excuses, self-pity, and negative thinking. We can choose to be pity-filled or hope-filled through our Blessed Hope—Jesus Christ.

For many years I had a poster on my wall which was given to me by an acquaintance. It was a picture of a small child sitting in his highchair. Tears were running down his face. On top of his head was his overturned bowl of spaghetti. Underneath the image was a statement based on Psalm 118:24, "This is the day the Lord has made, I will rejoice and be glad in it." My prayer each day is this: "God you have given me another day, help me to treasure it and use it wisely."

In Summary

Remember, we do not have to kick down the doors of opportunity. We only have to move quickly with determination through the doors that God opens for us. At times we spend a lot of energy to force open doors that God has not opened, when instead we should spend more time seeking God's will for our lives. When we do that, we will be prepared when the door opens, and we can seize the opportunity that God has placed before us.

Chapter Three

Leaders Realize Their Potential

I can do all things through Christ which strengtheneth me.
—Philippians 4:13

If you only read the first part of Philippians 4:13 cited above, you would think you were reading about an egomaniac. Nothing could be further from the truth. The apostle Paul, who penned those words while in prison, was a man who knew that Jesus Christ was the source of his strength. In the early months of my ministry work, I sought after books on self-confidence. I come from a rural background. I had very little exposure to public speaking or being in a place of leadership. I wanted to learn all I could about self-confidence. It seemed to me that if I would be leading people, then I would need all the confidence I could muster. Then one day I read the Scripture, "I can do all things through Christ which strengtheneth me." Suddenly a light went on in my head. I realized that I did not need more self-confidence but more God-confidence. This did not preclude doing everything I could to improve myself. I studied the lives of great leaders, listened to the tapes of great speakers and even went to the best department store in my small town and asked the manager to teach me all he could about how to dress and how to match colors. I did not want to limit myself in any way.

I wanted to be my best, all the while realizing that I had God on my side to strengthen me. Whatever you do, whether it is in business, education, counseling or ministry, you should consult with God and get His leadership. Once you apply His direction to your life you can "pull out all the stops," knowing that He will help you succeed. We see that the message in 1 John 4:4b reminds us that "...greater is He that is in us than he that is in the world."

Anytime you attempt something great—something worthwhile, you can rest assured that you will face opposition. Sometimes it will come from an outside force. Sometimes it will come from those who are closest to you—individuals you would expect to be your allies. Mankind is endowed with far greater potential than any other living creature—because he is made in the image and likeness of God.

> "Ye are of God, little children, and have overcome them: because greater is he that is in you, than he that is in the world." —1 John 4:4

In Psalm 139:14 King David said, "I will give thanks to Thee, for I am fearfully and wonderfully made. Dr. Earl Williams makes this interesting point:

The center piece of man's natural physical being is his brain through which his spiritual being (the mind and soul) functions. The brain is the most complex, mysterious organ in the universe. It only weighs about three pounds in a healthy adult and we are informed by brain specialists that it is composed of billions of cells and electrical connections.

It is by using the brain that mankind can reason, make decisions, communicate thoughts and most of all—have the ability to commune with God. The songwriter, Bill Gaither, said it well when he wrote these words in one of his songs, "I am a promise, I am a possibility." We should never be afraid to demand great things of ourselves. God made you with the potential for greatness. Self-confidence (God-confidence) is essential for those who are to succeed in life.

We cannot expect other people to have confidence in our abilities unless we display it in ourselves. Our Creator has made us reservoirs of His power. Dr. Orison S. Marden was an inspirational American author in the late 1800s and early 1900s. In 1897 he founded a magazine titled, *Success.* He wrote these words of wisdom:

> If we only better understood our spiritual resources, we would have a larger faith. We are crippled by the old idea of man's inferiority. There is no inferiority about the man God made once we get this matter of sin settled—which is done through Jesus Christ, the Redeemer. The only inferiority then is what we put into ourselves.

I frequently meet people who emphasize their excuses for failure (e.g., born into a poor family, not enough education, mistreated, misunderstood, can't get a break or are unappreciated). Why not eliminate those negative thoughts and rise to the potential God has given you? So many people spend their entire lives seeking someone or something to blame. Most often they go all the way back to childhood, and attach all their later failures on the fact that they came from a poor beginning and did not have the same benefits as others.

If you are a child of God, you put an end to your past when you were born-again by the Spirit of God. The Bible says, "Therefore if any man be in Christ, he is a new creature: old things are passed away; behold, all things are become new" (2 Corinthians 5:17). A careful study of people who rose to success will show that a large number of them came from very obscure beginnings. Poverty and broken homes marked the beginning for some of yesterday's and today's greatest success stories. I always have the perfect answer for people who would seek excuses instead of solutions—my own testimony.

While I come from a very happy home with loving Christian parents, money was always in short supply. Because we lived on a farm and raised much of our own food, there was never a time when we were without, but it was very seldom that my brother or I had much money. Of course we did not know we were poor, as everyone else around us was as well. We accepted our lifestyle as our way of life. Until I was about 10 or 12 years old, we did not have indoor plumbing. I still remember going to the outdoor bathroom on cold dark winter nights.

Most of the time during my high school days I had only one or two pairs of blue jeans. This often necessitated washing them out at night and hanging them up to dry. The next morning the pockets would still be wet and I would try to iron them dry. When I would go out front to catch the school bus, and hopefully sit by a certain girl—my pants would steam in the cool morning air. It is difficult to be a "cool" guy when you are sitting there with steam rising off your semi-dry trousers.

Having completed high school, I faced the challenge of how to raise the funds to attend college. As I said earlier, it never occurred to me that I wouldn't go, and during the summer months I took every odd job I could find from picking strawberries to cleaning out stock barns. When school started, I delivered papers from 4:00 a.m. to 6:00 a.m. This gave me just enough money to get by.

Because I was unable to afford living in a dorm, I rented a sleeping room for $20 per month (this was in 1959). While the room had no kitchen, in the winter I was able to do most of my cooking on the old cast iron steam radiator that heated the room. By putting food in small pans on the radiator while I was in class, I would return in the afternoon to a nice hot meal. I still remember those days with a smile. They were not hardships, but challenges that helped build my character.

Most of us can find an excuse if we choose to (e.g. poor beginnings, mistreatment by someone, cheated by someone, bad breaks or just poor judgment). We are all better off when we put away those excuses and determine that we will use those past hardships and injustices as character building blocks instead of road blocks to future success. Realizing your full potential is not a destination but a journey which lasts throughout your entire lifetime. It requires both patience and persistence. Do not always try to bulldoze your way through opposition. Sometimes with a little persuasion, those who originally opposed you can be converted and become your greatest helpers. God has a way of making things right when we stay out of His way.

Everyone has potential. Of course some people are more gifted than others. Normally, we would expect individuals who are most gifted and most intelligent to be the ones to excel and become great successes. Many times this is true—but not always. All of us know someone or have heard of someone who was not especially gifted or intelligent; but through hard work, perseverance and utilizing confidence in God's leading—became a great success. I have always admired people like that. I look at them and realize that we all have potential. I see that we all have the opportunity to excel in one way or another.

Scientists tell us that we only use 10 percent or less of the brain. I do not believe when God created us and gave us each a brain, that He intended only a mere 10 percent of it to be used. If we are able to at least get up to 12.5 percent that would put us 25 percent ahead of the crowd. We should be challenged to reach our potential in all things. Unfortunately, most of us are satisfied with the status quo and stay in our limited comfort zones. If we are to reach our God-given potential, we must at times, challenge the status quo and move past our ordinary and familiar routines.

We all have certain routines that we go through each day. I have a particular routine I follow every morning; I brush my teeth, shower, shave and blow dry my hair in twenty minutes or less. I have it down to a science. There are certain things that we do over and over exactly the same way. Observe yourself for a few days. Most people will always tie the same shoe first.

It's all right if we do some things the same way all the time in a mindless routine. The problem comes when we allow our entire lives to become one mindless routine. Eventually, routine kills motivation and thwarts our potential to reach God's best for us. The late Warren Bennis, founder of the Leadership Institute at the University of Southern California and co-author of the popular book, *Leaders*, describes how routines prevented change when he was president of the University of Cincinnati:

> My moment of truth came toward the end of my first ten months. It was one of those nights in the office. The clock was moving toward four in the morning, and I was still not finished with the incredible mass of paper stacked before me. I was bone weary and soul weary and I found myself muttering, "Either I can't manage this place, or it's unmanageable." I reached for my calendar and ran my eyes down each hour, half-hour, quarter-hour to see where my time had gone that day, the day before, the month before... My discovery was this: I had become the victim of a vast, amorphous, unwitting, unconscious conspiracy to prevent me from doing anything whatever, to change the university's status quo.

Bennis coined a phrase to describe this self-defeating phenomenon, "Bennis' First Law of Academic Pseudodynamics - routine work drives out non-routine work and smothers to death all creative planning." This statement can apply to all fundamental changes at a university or any institution. Every executive we know can relate to the dilemma described by Warren Bennis.

In their book, *Leadership Challenge*, the authors James Kouzes and Barry Posner, point out that routines can get us into ruts. Routines dull our senses. Routines stifle our creativity, constrict our thinking, remove us from stimulation and destroy our ability to compete. We get in life what we will accept. If you are willing to accept the mediocre, the broken, the less than best—then that is probably what you will have. On the other hand, if you are willing to put aside excuses and commit yourself to achieve your God-given potential, it may be surprising what you can accomplish. Our lives are made up of decisions. Every day we are bombarded with all kinds of decisions, both great and small. Sometimes a single decision will set the course for the remainder of our lives.

As you search for personal achievement and fulfillment in life, do not look for a miracle—because quite probably you will not find it. But you *can* find principles of success that will lead to personal success. Those principles are available to all who have the courage to find and use them. Individuals who can make decisions promptly and decisively, know what they want and will generally get it. Indecisive or negative thinking will generally produce the opposite outcome. Zig Ziglar often terms it "Stinking Thinking."

Successful people are usually known for their concentration of purpose. The Bible uses the term "single mindedness." They have one thought or goal in mind. Successful people are usually those who have been able to focus all their intellect and abilities on one pursuit or one goal, until they have accomplished it. The late pastor and Bible teacher, Dr. J. Herbert Randall once said:

> Any individual can be, in time, what he earnestly desires to be, if he but sets his face steadfastly in the direction of that thing and brings all his powers to bear upon its attainment. It is impossible for anyone to be successful in every branch of business, or renowned in every department of a professional life. We must learn to bend or focus our energies to one point, and go directly to that point, looking neither to the right not the left.

In Summary

Remember that God makes everyone special. This truth has been taught for ages, but only in recent years with the development of DNA studies have we become aware of just how accurate that statement is. God has given you specific gifts and talents. We do not all have the same talents.

My daughter, Kim, has the gift of determination. As a high school freshman she tried out for cheerleading. When she wasn't chosen she was crushed. She began to practice every day. She did so many round-offs in our living room that the floors creaked.

The following year she won first place trophy in the Tri-State cheerleading competition. That determination has served her well. She is now a highly respected business leader in Knoxville, Tennessee and is Vice President/CEO of the Knoxville Academy of Medicine.

My son, Scott, is a gifted musician. He is a natural but he perfected that gift until there is virtually nothing in the field of music that he cannot do. Oh, how I have wished that I had that gift, but I can't play a single instrument. I am not responsible for that gift, but the gifts that God has given me *are* my responsibility. All of us are responsible to God to develop and refine what He has given specifically to us—so we can accomplish all that God expects of us.

"There are no Lone Ranger leaders. Think about it; if you are alone, you are not leading anybody, are you?"
—John Maxwell

Chapter Four

Leaders Develop Their Leadership Potential

Study to shew thyself approved unto God, a workman that needeth not to be ashamed, rightly dividing the word of truth.
—2 Timothy 2:15

All good organizations must have a strong, effective leader. While some organizations have succeeded with shared leadership—the vast majority of institutions are headed by one dedicated, focused, talented and dynamic leader. The late Dr. Lee Robertson, who was the chancellor of Tennessee Temple University is remembered for his often quoted remark, "Everything rises and falls on leadership."

Dr. Ed Young, pastor of the great Second Baptist Church in Houston, Texas, speaking to a group of preachers—challenged the men to provide their churches with these three things: leadership, leadership, and leadership. Successful leaders have high expectations, both of themselves and of their followers.

These expectations are powerful, because they are the frames into which people fit reality.

In this way, you see what you expect to see, rather than what may be actually occurring. Social psychologists have referred to this as the Pygmalion effect, based on a Greek myth about Pygmalion—a sculptor who carved a statue of a beautiful woman, fell in love with the statue, and brought it to life by the strength of his perceptions. Leaders play Pygmalion-like roles in developing people.

The effectiveness of a leader comes not so much from what that individual accomplishes alone, but from the effectiveness of the team that he or she builds in order to accomplish specific goals. In the mid to late 1990s, the catch phrase of organizational management was "team building." Certainly this has proven to be an effective form of organization, especially when dealing with today's sophisticated, well-educated and technologically literate work force. Establishing teams in no way diminishes the need for structured decisive and dynamic leadership. Teams and strong effective leadership go together. Teams integrate and enhance formal structures and processes.

Hierarchical structures and basic leadership processes are essential to large organizations and need not be threatened by teams. Teams, in fact, are the best way to integrate across structural boundaries, design and energize core processes. Those who see teams as a replacement for hierarchy are missing the true potential of teams. Teams are a way of enhancing performance and increasing productivity.

Managers cannot master the opportunities and challenges confronting them without emphasizing the need for well-organized teams. In today's market, this is needed more than ever before. The performance challenges that large companies face in every industry such as customer service, technological change, competitive threats, and environmental constraints—demand the kind of responsiveness, speed, on-line customization and quality that is beyond the reach of mere individual performance. Well-trained teams can bridge that gap. Andrew J. DuBrin points out four benefits of effective leadership:

Respect and Status
A leader frequently receives respect from group members. He or she also enjoys a higher status than people who are not occupying a leadership role. Status accompanies being appointed to a leadership position on or off the job. When an individual's personal qualifications match the position, his or her status is even higher.

A Feeling of Power and Prestige
Being a leader automatically grants you some power. Prestige is forthcoming because many people think highly of people who are leaders. In many organizations, top-level leaders are addressed as Mr., Mrs. or Ms.; whereas lower-ranking people are referred to by their surnames.

A Chance to Help Others
A leader works directly with people, often teaching them job skills, serving as a mentor and listening to personal problems. Part of a leader's job is to help other people become managers and leaders. A leader often feels as much of a "people helper" as does a human resources manager or a counselor.

High Income

Leaders, in general, receive higher pay than team members, and executive leaders in major business corporations typically earn several million dollars per year. If money is an important motivator or satisfier, being a leader has a built-in satisfaction. In some situations a team leader earns virtually the same amount of money as other team members. Occupying a leadership position, however, is a starting point on the path to high-paying leadership positions.

While leadership philosophy has greatly changed in most progressive forward thinking organizations, I find that most leaders of religious groups or churches generally ascribe to a much older leadership model. They tend to fall into one of three basic leadership styles. Their leadership will be one of these three styles:

- Autocratic; the rigidly controlling sort.
- A democratic leader who asks others for opinions and suggestions.
- A laissez-faire leader who takes little action to influence the group.

While leaders may use a combination of all three styles, most leaders use one style more than the others. Autocratic leadership requires that all authority centers around one person. Communication tends to primarily flow in one direction from the leader to the managers and staff.

This style requires conformity and obedience on the part of the followers. Autocratic leadership has an advantage in the speed with which decisions can be made. This can be effective in the short-term and is decidedly beneficial in start-up companies and small institutions. The down side of autocratic leadership is that it fails to utilize the talents and ideas of the rest of the management team.

Autocratic leadership also has a tendency to cause low group morale. Autocratic leaders who do not ask for help or seek suggestions from others within the institution become vulnerable to mistakes that could have been avoided. They tend to have blind followers.

In religious circles, the autocratic leader has a tendency to form opinions and attribute them to God's instruction. The leader God has placed in authority must pay careful attention that God has really spoken, and that he or she is not just giving divine attributes to personal firmly held preferences and opinions.

Democratic leadership is a stark contrast to the autocratic style. Democratic or participative leadership takes into consideration the wishes and suggestions of other members of the administrative team. Advantages of democratic leadership include better morale and more support when making final decisions. Properly implemented participative leadership ultimately results in better decisions regarding the direction that the institution will take.

Potential disadvantages of democratic leadership include a stagnant process that is never able to come to concise conclusions on how the institution will operate. This can be avoided when the leader has the confidence to be both flexible and forceful. That leader must have the ability to take the ideas of others and then give them form and function.

Laissez-faire leadership takes the position of "Let them do their own thing." While this allows an opportunity for individual development, it usually leads to a very fragmented organization. Seldom is a leader so blessed as to have a staff that can operate without structure. One is reminded of the old adage, "Do not expect, inspect."

Leaders Must Be Visionaries

Effective leaders, literally, must see *what* they are working toward *before* it exists, and then create the process and function to see it come to pass. The true visionary is one who takes action to make that envisioned idea become a reality. Many who claim the title of "visionary" are actually dreamers who sit around building air castles that never develop into anything.

The true visionary leader does not simply dream a dream and announce it; but instead, refines that vision and has a realistic plan of action before he or she reveals the plan. Others who act too quickly usually have a career of failed projects that not only damage the institution but lead to a distinct loss of confidence in their leadership.

I was once told about an incident that happened at the dedication of Disney World in Orlando, Florida. Walt Disney was already deceased and several honored guests were present. As one guest spoke he turned and said, "I just wish Walt could have seen this." An associate stepped to the microphone and said, "Oh, but he did. He saw it first." Virtually all worthwhile projects begin in the mind of a visionary leader who conceives the idea and then begins to implement the policy, personnel and provisions to make it come to pass.

Dr. George Flanagan in his dissertation, *Profiles in Leadership,* says: "Leaders who lack vision are simply caretakers, gatekeepers and time savers. Leaders accomplish the organization's mission by providing vision. Vision assists the leaders in developing, planning, and implementing change."

Leaders Set High Standards

In most everything of consequence in life there is a standard. In Washington D.C. there is a place called the Bureau of Standards. There, we find the fixed standard for most everything of consequence in the physical world. For instance, how do we know what constitutes a pound?

The Bureau of Standards gives us the answer – 16 ounces equals one pound. How do we know how far is a mile? The bureau gives us the answer – 5,280 feet equals one mile. What is the standard for time? How do we know the correct time of day? The Bureau of Standards in Washington D.C. has technical equipment which measures the movement of the planets in our solar system that determine the time of day at any point on planet Earth.

Key time keeping instruments on earth are adjusted at regular intervals with this standard for time produced in the Bureau of

Standards in Washing D.C. When standards are established and emphasized, everyone can take pride in both accomplishments and the style of operation. Assisting and supporting members of a staff through times of professional and personal crisis helps establish dignity.

Leaders Must Be Reliable and Consistent

Again, quoting from *Profiles in Leadership,* "Reliability enables leaders to provide stability and strength to organizations. Important aspects of reliability are persistence and consistency. Leaders must balance commitments so as they do not over commit and adversely affect their reliability." Good leaders tend to have charisma and a personality that is termed "leadership style."

Leadership style involves the ability to influence in a desired direction. The leader must be a motivator who brings out both inspiration and dedication of their staff. Leadership style should bring forth both confidence and a sense of well-being in the organization. There must be a feeling within the crew that the ship is in the hands of an intelligent, educated, disciplined and dedicated captain.

Leaders must never display traits of pettiness or lack of integrity. The leader must be an example of solidarity in times of stress. Leaders must inspire confidence, loyalty and unfailing dedication from those who must follow their leadership. When leadership is confident and solid, the organization moves ahead. When leadership is uncertain, confusion reigns and anarchy appears.

Leaders Must Demonstrate an Extraordinary Value System

The integrity of a leader must be above question. He or she must radiate an unselfish attitude toward the well-being of both the organization and the staff. This ability, to put the well-being of others first, generates a feeling of security and admiration among subordinates.

Integrity is not living by principles, but the process of *choosing* the principles by which to live. Honesty, consistency, and morality should be the result of such choices. In simple terms, the leader is to be believed. He or she not only does not lie, but also does not allow misleading statements and half-truths to exist. A leader does not turn a blind eye or deaf ear to mistruths or dishonest acts so that later he or she has deniability.

Leaders Must Be Good Communicators

Failure to properly communicate your ideas will cause failure in leadership, and ultimately failure within the organization. Often in staff meetings, I discuss the concept of corporate culture. Corporate culture, simply stated, means that the entire staff is pointed in the same direction; that everyone is on the same page.

In a growing organization it becomes more difficult to maintain proper lines of communication. Each time a staff member is added, the dynamics of communication change. For example, in a small two-person company there is often the greatest opportunity for direct conversation and discussion throughout the day, thereby achieving quick, easy and descriptive communication.

If, however, a third member is added to the team, then six possible lines of communication are created—an increase of

300 percent. Direct communication becomes more difficult, and often messages are interpreted (or misinterpreted) in a variety of different ways. Now, add a fourth team member and your communication possibilities increase to 12.

A fifth person increases the possibilities to 20. That's 20 different ways a message can be sent and interpreted. At this point, failure to communicate can occur. Communication must become more formal; and written memos, formal requests, etc. become part of daily operations. The following chart shows how much more complex communication becomes each time a new member is added to a team.

1 2

2 people - 2 possibilities

2

1 3

3 people - 6 possibilities

2

3 4

4 people - 12 possibilities

1

2 3

4 5

5 people - 20 possibilities

Leaders Must Be Effective Decision Makers

Leaders must gather pertinent data and reach conclusions. Having reached a decision, the leader must then put that decision into action. Leaders understand that decisions are of little value if they are not implemented and supported by an appropriate follow-up policy.

One of Henry Ford's most outstanding qualities was his habit of reaching decisions quickly and definitely; and making changes slowly. This quality was so pronounced in Mr. Ford that it gave him the reputation of being obstinate. It was this fast decision making quality which prompted him to continue the manufacturing of his famous Model T Ford, the world's ugliest car, when all of his advisors and many purchasers of the car were urging him to change its design.

Perhaps Mr. Ford delayed too long in making the change. But it is evident that his firmness of decision yielded a huge fortune before the change in the model became necessary. There can be little doubt that Henry Ford's habit of definiteness of decision assumed the proportions of obstinacy, but quality is preferable to slowness in reaching decisions and quickness in changing them.

Leaders Must Be Team Builders

The success and effectiveness of a leader is determined by the efficiency of the team surrounding that leader. Team building leaders make it possible for all group members to work together, and help the group move from an adversarial silo management relationship—to a collaborative one. They provide the substance that holds the team together. Productive staff meetings are a key component in developing a team spirit.

Leaders Meet with All Team Members As a Group

Periodically, the leader must pull together all members of the team. Leaders must choose a designated time to convey important messages such as new policies, changes in implementation of policies, etc. If at all possible, these group staff meetings should take place when there are few distractions. For example, when office machines are shut down or when the phones aren't ringing.

How to Present Long or Complex Messages

In this case, first present your message verbally, then distribute written copies of your verbal message. This technique increases retention and understanding. When holding staff meetings always provide a quick review of what has transpired since the last meeting, and what your expectations are before the next one.

By having regular scheduled meetings, each team member will know that he or she will be briefed on all company matters that pertain to them. Keeping all staff members informed and updated on relevant issues ensures that your team members can function smoothly, effectively and at their optimum level.

Leaders Must Inspire and Require Excellence

Four decades ago, Tom Peters wrote a book titled, *In Search of Excellence.* It became a best seller and "in search of excellence" became a catch phrase of many corporations. While many new books by Tom Peters and others have been written, and the term "search for excellence" may seem a little dated, certainly the theme is not. Our goal is still to strive to create excellence in all that we do—simply to be the best.

Occasionally, on Saturdays, I enjoy going to the local Waffle House restaurant for breakfast. While the restaurant makes no claim to perfection, they are good at what they do—frying eggs. I enjoy watching the grill man as he flips the eggs high above his frying pan, and with the sure handedness of a pro-athlete—catches them without incident or accident. I have often used him as an example in my lectures.

If your lot in life is to fry eggs, then be the best egg fryer in the business. That philosophy should be true whatever your calling may be in life. This is especially true of those called into the Lord's work—whether it be as a minister, educator, youth minister, minister of music or general staff worker, do your best. If you are the janitor of the Lord's house, then that church should have the cleanest rest rooms in town. Whatever your calling is, treat it as if it is the greatest work on earth; we should accept nothing less than excellence.

When I came to Louisiana Baptist University, I wrote for materials from some of the nation's best non-traditional schools. I invested the time and expense to personally visit some of the nation's best. I asked questions. I took notes and all the samples they would give me. Careful research was made of the schools that have demonstrated that they have a capacity to graduate excellent students. While we should not simply copy someone else, we should have enough common sense to look at their success and learn some important aspects of what makes an excellent school.

The goal of both my staff and myself has never been numbers, but excellence. We very seldom discuss numbers. Of course we do have some general numerical goals, but they are very soft goals. The conversation in our staff meetings and in daily office communication is usually centered on quality and excellence. We really want everything we do to be first class. We have a small, dedicated staff that really cares. Those who are not driven to excellence usually quickly eliminate themselves.

Leaders Must Develop the Right Kind of Philosophy

Leaders must be guided by a specific set of deeply held convictions; those convictions must determine all that we do. Convictions are very different from preferences. Compromises and accommodations can be adjusted but truly held convictions can never be compromised. A person's behavior is guided by his or her deepest convictions and beliefs, determining what action will be taken.

A Christian philosophy is built first of all on the acceptance of a Divine Creator, God Almighty. From Him emanates all truth and knowledge. Therefore, all action must be built on this foundation. Christian philosophy is built on an acceptance of the need for a Redeemer, and that Man cannot redeem himself. This is a radical difference from the secular humanist position that mankind is innately good—that through more education and social engineering, humanity can become all that society desires.

Leaders Must Take Care to Live Balanced Lives

Dr. George Flanagan states, "Principle-centered leaders are active socially and they have many friends and a few confidants. They are active intellectually and physically. Their actions and attitudes are proportionate to the situation; balanced, temperate, moderate and wise." Leaders should be aware of the important place that proper mental and physical health plays in good leadership. No one enjoys sound physical health for a long period of time without developing health consciousness. This is true of both mental and physical fitness.

We must banish worry and fear by maintaining a positive mental attitude. If we are to maintain a healthy consciousness, fear and worry should have no place in your life; they undermine good health. Learn the habit of emotional control. Emotions such as malice, revenge and resentment produce toxins or poisons in the blood. Maintain a positive mental attitude at all times, for in doing so a healthful influence will be produced. All thought energy, whether it is positive or negative, is carried to all parts of the body. Attitude affects blood pressure, digestion and the body's ability to heal itself.

The physical body is a temple that God has provided to serve as a dwelling place for the mind and spirit. It is the most perfect living organism ever developed. If we are to function properly as leaders, we must give great care to properly maintain our bodies through proper rest and nutrition. If our health is bad and we become ill and irritable, we impair our ability to lead. As I get older I become more aware of the need to take care of my physical body. While I am no paragon of physical fitness, I do try to make it to the gym three or four times a week, and have reduced my weight by over twenty pounds.

Most dietary problems stem from eating too much refined and processed foods, fatty foods, stimulating or intoxicating foods and food additives. Such foods are deficient in essential vitamins and minerals—they are too high in sugar, and they lack fiber or roughage essential for healthy elimination.

God's Word seems to bear out the fact that we really are what we eat. Yet, most of us are prone to bypass healthy foods and grab a quick hamburger or some other fat saturated food. God placed a high value on the human body when he said, "Do you not know that your body is the temple of the Holy Spirit…you are not your own; you are bought with a price, so glorify God in your body" (1 Corinthians 6:19-20).

Good Leaders Must Be Self-Encouraging

Leaders tend to have many acquaintances but few close friends in which they confide. It therefore becomes necessary to be self-encouraging. It is said of David in the Bible that he encouraged himself (1 Samuel 30:6). It is essential for the principle-centered leader to renew all four dimensions of the human personality: Physical, mental, emotional, and spiritual.

This requires the right, healthy diet, exercise, appropriate rest and attention to the spiritual aspect of our lives. Perhaps this area is the most neglected among leaders. Failure to take time for self-renewal causes burn-out, fatigue, emotional and physical illness. It is significant that even Christ at times attempted to come apart from the crowds. Evangelist Vance Havner said it well, "Come apart or come apart."

No chapter on leadership would be complete without discussing why leaders fail. It is just as essential to know what not to do as what to do. While there are many contributing factors, we will deal with just a few of the most blatant ones that contribute to failure:

First, a lack of honesty or integrity.

The leader must be above reproach. Leaders must be trustworthy to the highest degree. Truly effective leaders must nurture trust at all levels in the organization. Their word must be their bond.

Second, an inability to organize details.

Efficient leadership calls for the ability to organize and master details. Leaders need to prioritize and do first things first. Executives must not only understand the major elements of their business; they must keep up with changes. The successful leader must be the master of all details connected with his or her position. That means, of course, that a leader must acquire the habit of relegating details to capable lieutenants.

Third, the misuse of authority.

The effective leader leads through encouragement and inspiration, and not by trying to instill fear in the hearts of his or her followers. The leader who tries to impress followers with his or her "authority" comes within the category of "leadership through force." If a leader is a real leader, he or she will have no need to advertise that fact except by his or her outstanding conduct.

Fourth, arrogance.

Truly great leaders are willing, when occasion demands, to perform any sort of labor which they would ask another to perform. "But he that is greatest among you shall be your servant" (Matthew 23:11). The leader who claims all the honor for the work of his or her followers is sure to be met by resentment. A really great leader claims none of the honors. A great leader is content to see the honors—when there are any, go to his or her followers, knowing that most people will work harder for commendation and recognition than they will for money alone. Great leaders are servants to the organization and those who work under him/her.

Fifth, greed.

All great leaders, be it religious or secular, always place the interest of the organization first. An effective leader does not enter into a program for personal gratification and advancement—but because it is best for the church, university, or business. While it is appropriate that the leader be properly compensated for good leadership, most people know of instances where the compensation far outdistances the quality of the leadership.

Sixth, failure to delegate.

Dr. Earl Williams makes this important point:

> The leader who fears that one of his followers may take his position is practically sure to realize that fear sooner or later. The able leader trains understudies to whom he or she may delegate, at will, any of the details of position. Only in this way may a leader multiply himself and prepare himself to be at many places, and give attention to many things at one time.

> It is an eternal truth that men receive more pay for their ability to get others to perform, than they could possibly earn by their own efforts. An efficient leader may, through his knowledge of the job and the magnetism of his personality, greatly increase the efficiency of others, and induce them to render more service and better service than they could render without his aid.

I have a beautiful color print on my office wall. It is a photograph of a soaring eagle. Underneath is the caption, "Leaders are like eagles, they don't flock, you find them one at a time."

In Summary

Being a leader is a special calling. Leadership brings with it special blessings and rewards. But leadership also brings awesome responsibility. Anyone who aspires to a position of leadership must also be willing to accept the responsibility of that position. Leaders must set high standards for themselves, standards of integrity, honesty, self-sacrifice and hard work.

Never ask those who under you to do what you yourself are not willing to do. Realize that leaders are servants; servants to those under them, servants to the organization they represent, servants to the people that the organization serves and most of all—servants to Christ. One only needs to look to the character of Christ to find the perfect example of servant leadership.

Servant leadership is not just about being nice. It really works. True servant leaders must first demonstrate that they truly care about the church or institution and the people they lead. This creates trust and trust creates productivity.

Chapter Five

Leaders Change the Paradigms

He that observeth the wind shall not sow; and he that regardeth the clouds shall not reap.
— Ecclesiastes 11:4

According to Joel Arthur Baker, the first person to popularize the concept of paradigm shifts in the corporate world, a paradigm is a set of rules and regulations (written or nonwritten) that does two things: Establishes or defines boundaries and tells you how to behave inside the boundaries in order to be successful. In other words, a paradigm means doing something the same way over and over—rejecting new thinking and new ways of doing things and to follow old traditions without asking why.

> "To everything there is a season, and a time to every purpose under the heaven: A time to be born, and a time to die; a time to plant, and a time to pluck up that which is planted; a

> time to kill, and a time to heal; a time to break down, and a time to build up; a time to weep, and a time to laugh; a time to mourn, and a time to dance; a time to cast away stones, and a time to gather stones together; a time to embrace, and a time to refrain from embracing; a time to get, and a time to lose; a time to keep, and a time to cast away; a time to rend, and a time to sew; a time to keep silence, and a time to speak; a time to love, and a time of peace" (Ecclesiastes 3:1-8).

I heard a story many years ago about a young couple. They had just settled into their new home, and the bride wanted to fix a very special dinner for her newlywed husband. She decided she would bake him a ham. He watched as she got out the pan, selected all the spices and began to prepare the ham. Just before she placed it in the pan she took a sharp knife and cut approximately two inches off the end of the ham.

With curiosity he asked, "Why did you cut off the end of the ham?" She answered, "I don't know, that is the way my mother did it." So they decided to call her mother to find out. Her mother answered, "I don't know but I will call your grandmother to find out." When she called her mother and asked why she cut two inches off the ham before she baked it, she answered, "Oh, it's because I never had a pan large enough to bake a ham." So, for two generations the end was cut off the ham because the first lady did not have a large enough pan. It sounds ridiculous but many times we do things that are just as much without merit.

In 1968, more than 65 percent of the unit sales in the world were Swiss made watches. Eighty to ninety percent of the profit of all watch sales went to the Swiss watchmakers. Yet by 1980, their market share had dropped from 65 percent to less than

10 percent. What happened? Swiss watchmakers had run into a paradigm shift. The mechanical watch was about to give way to the electronic watch. All the things that the Swiss were good at such as making springs, bearings and gears were quickly becoming irrelevant. In less than ten years, the Swiss watch market would be destroyed causing 50,000 of the 62,000 Swiss watchmakers to become unemployed.

The nation of Japan caught a windfall; the electronic quartz watch was a natural for a country just developing in the electronic field. At the beginning of the paradigm shift, barely one percent of the world's watchmakers were Japanese. Soon, they controlled the world market. The irony is that the Swiss invented the electronic quartz movement in a research institute in Newchatel, Switzerland. When the Swiss researchers presented the revolutionary new idea to the Swiss manufacturers in 1967, it was rejected.

The well-respected Swiss watchmakers had a long-established way of making watches and were unwilling to change. After all, they had proven themselves to be the best watchmakers in the entire world. They could not see the paradigm shift that was about to take place, and were virtually eliminated from the world market while they held on to their old ways. What is a paradigm? The dictionary tells us it comes from the Greek word *paradeigma*, meaning model, pattern or example.

Thomas Kuhn states that scientific paradigms are "accepted examples of actual scientific practice, examples which include law, theory, application, and instrumentation together – (that) provide models from which spring particular coherent traditions of scientific research." He adds, "Men whose research is based on shared paradigms are committed to the same rules and standards for scientific practice." (In other words, they are resistant to change.) Adam Smith's definition of paradigm, in his book, *Powers of the Mind* is this:

> A shared set of assumptions. The paradigm is the way we perceive the world; water to the fish. The paradigm explains the world to us and helps us to predict its behavior." Smith's point about prediction is important. We will see that most of the time we do not predict things with our paradigms. But paradigms do give us the added advantage of being able to create a valid set of expectations about what will probably occur in the world based on our shared set of assumptions. "When we are in the middle of the paradigm," Smith concludes, "it is hard to imagine any other paradigm."

One of the problems with Thomas Kuhn's book, *Structure of Scientific Revolutions*, is the insistence that paradigms exist only in science. There is great evidence that paradigm shifts are not only controlled by science, but also by the human condition. Author, Joel Baker, points out some of those human condition paradigm shifts:

> When we look back to the 1960s, we see nonscientific paradigm shifts: Parents responded so violently to drugs and long hair on their children because these things represented a cultural paradigm shift; we missed the OPEC revolution because of an economic paradigm shift. Our country's inability to understand the Iranian revolution had to do with religious paradigms. Much of the confusion we have about the future is because of changes in paradigms.

These paradigm changes are especially important for all of us because whether it is in business, education, politics or our personal lives, a paradigm change—by definition, alters the basic rules of the game. When do paradigms change? When someone breaks through established barriers or develops a better plan.

Until recently, many artificial limits were established in sports as to how high someone could jump, how much weight could be lifted or how fast someone could run the mile. It was a commonly held fact that no one could run the mile in less than four minutes. Then Roger Bannister broke the paradigm. Now it has been broken many times by different runners.

Perhaps never before in history has a more revolutionary change taken place than in the computer industry. The invention of the computer itself started a revolution of change, but what has happened within that new industry is even more revolutionary. It has created more wealth and has drastically changed how the world operates, more so than any other industry in the 20th century. In less than two decades, it too, has changed its paradigms—more than a few times.

In the beginning of the computer surge, all computers were large mainframes. Sometimes they took up entire buildings. IBM controlled the market. "Big Blue" was such a giant that many thought they would control the market and drive out competitors for years, maybe even decades to come. Then, two men got together in their garage and developed the Apple computer. Almost overnight the paradigm shifted again, to personal computers. IBM was slow to react, and for awhile, Apple flooded the market.

When IBM responded with their own personal computer, Apple refused to make theirs compatible and chose to go it alone. They believed they had a superior product, and in the beginning, they probably did. But soon, other hardware was developed and improved. Enter Bill Gates and Microsoft, and other software companies that were not compatible with Apple; again change took place. Apple diminished and Bill Gates became one of the world's richest men.

Not only was there change in the computers, but also in the marketing. Two decades ago, Michael Dell, a technology student at the University of Texas, came up with the idea that computers could be sold over the phone. Up until that time, computers had been sold primarily in stores much like a refrigerator or television. Customers would come in, view the merchandise and purchase a computer based on a number of factors. Dell believed that he could find a better way to sell his customized computers using telephone sales. The idea was that instead of making up a standard, one size fits all computer, the customer would call in and order a computer that fit their personal needs. Within 48 hours the custom made model would be assembled and shipped.

From a meager start, the company skyrocketed and Dell became one of the most profitable companies in computer history. At one point stock was up a staggering 29,600 percent. By that time, Apple stock had pretty well tanked. They were not considered a major player anymore. Then Apple came up with a new product, the iPod. It was an overnight sensation. Apple stock suddenly soared again. And later, the Apple iPhone and its constant upgrades have made Apple one of the most profitable companies in history.

When consumers hold an Apple iPhone in their hands, they are holding more technology than we had in the Lunar Landing craft. Technology is now moving at the speed of light, and the public has an insatiable appetite for anything new. We may only be at the very edge of the technology age; where we may go with it in the next decade is a fascinating thought.

When a young elephant is born he is fixed with an ankle bracelet and chain and staked to the ground. In the beginning, he tries to break his chain again and again. After a while, he sees that he cannot break free. As he grows, the chain is only slightly increased in strength. The stake is also stronger, but only moderately. This giant mammal, weighing tons—could easily break the chain or pull out the stake but he never tries. In his mind he is trapped. There is no stronger prison known to mankind than the prison we build with our minds.

One of the funniest stories I ever heard describes a situation with two drunks. The first drunk had left a bar and on his way home decided to take a short cut through the cemetery. In the darkness he fell in to a freshly dug grave. For several minutes he tried to climb out but finally gave up. He decided to take a nap and wait for dawn. He leaned against one corner of the grave and was soon fast asleep.

A little later, a second drunk on his way home decided to take the same short cut and fell into the same grave. Unaware of the first drunk, he also tried desperately to climb out but had the same results. Just as he was about to give up trying to climb out, the noise made by the second drunk awakened the first drunk. In the darkness he reached out his hand and tapped the second man on the shoulder saying, "You can't get out." BUT HE DID!

Sometimes we just need the proper motivation. Someone has said that those who say, "It can't be done" are always being interrupted by those doing "it."

Change Is Usually Brought About By Some Type of Pressure

As long as we are comfortable in our existence, we are resistant to change. That is what happened with the Swiss watchmakers. They were the best, they controlled the market, and they were comfortable. Only after we have had to deal with some sort of setback—a physical or financial tragedy, are we forced into change. Change is usually brought about by one or more of the following: Friction, divorce, job loss, death in a family or having children.

In discussing friction, I often go to an illustration I learned while still in seminary. While I attended day classes, I worked the night shift at a local chair manufacturing factory. My job was to sand chair backs. Each night when I finished my shift, I was covered with close to an inch of very fine wood dust. In order to make production and draw a shift bonus we had to sand 1,000 chair backs in an eight-hour shift. This was done on a huge belt sander.

In order to reach production, we had to apply just the right amount of friction. If we jammed the wood against the sanders too hard, we would scorch the wood making it unusable. If we did not apply enough friction, it would take too long and we did not make production. I have discovered that life is a lot that way. If we push too hard, we destroy. But without friction, change will not take place.

Divorce is also a very powerful stimulus for change. When I was still in the pastorate, I often saw people who were in the process of divorce make radical changes. Some for the good but sadly many made changes for the worse. Death of a loved one often forces us to face change. Sometimes the change is emotional, but divorce can often result in both emotional and financial change. Loss of a job also brings on change. Sometimes it brings the tragic loss of home and financial security.

On the other hand, many times when someone is forced out of the comfort and security of a current job, a common response is to redirect his or her life's goals through re-education and/or relocation. It is also not uncommon to use the skills and knowledge already acquired to create a new product or start one's own company.

Having children also has its effect on change. Becoming parents forces us to make adjustments in life and refocus our priorities. James Dobson tells a story of a lady he met on a bus. She looked very tired and had dark circles under her eyes. She had seven kids with her. As she exited the bus he asked her, "Are all these children yours or are you on a picnic?" She answered, "Yes, they are all mine and believe me, it's no picnic." Most people will agree raising children is one of the toughest tasks in life. It is also one of the most important and rewarding.

Realize that temporary defeat can either crush us or make us stronger, and bring about needed changes in our life. If the first plan which you adopt does not work successfully, replace it with a new plan. If the second plan fails to work, modify it, change it or replace it with still another until you find a plan which docs work. It is at this point when most meet with failure because of the lack of persistence in creating new plans—to take the place of those which fail.

I recall walking through the great Landmark Baptist Temple when it was averaging 4,500 in attendance. The church's pastor, Dr. John Rawlings, was one of my heroes. He told me, "We often fail, but we have succeeded often enough to build what you see."

The most intelligent man alive cannot succeed in accumulating fame or fortune, or any other undertaking without plans that are practical and workable. Always keep that fact in mind. And remember, if a plan fails it is only a temporary defeat, not permanent failure. It may only mean that you plans were not sound and not carefully thought out. Build other plans! Start over again. Our "failures" can always be used to help perfect the next steps in our lives.

Millions of people go through life in misery and poverty because they lack a sound plan with which to reach intelligent goals. Your achievement cannot be greater than your plans are sound. As we enter into this new century, we stand on the doorstep of even more revolutionary change. Those who are going to thrive must anticipate those changes and take appropriate action. This is especially true of churches and other religious institutions.

Great changes have already taken place in the last twenty years. While some of those changes were needed and worthwhile, many were damaging and have left the Church weaker in many ways. One of the changes that took place was the rise of television evangelism. It has both a positive and negative effect. On the positive side, the gospel has been preached to millions and tens of thousands have been saved. Many who had never been exposed to the gospel were able to not only hear the gospel, but see the local church in action. But at its peak, negative things began to emerge.

With the public fall and humiliation of Jim Baker and Jimmy Swaggart, along with many other immoral and financial scandals, a new attitude set in toward Christianity. Televangelists and fundamentalists became the joke of late night talk shows. While

I applaud the legitimate religious programs, I personally feel that we have in some ways experienced a negative net effect on local church ministries. As we face the new millenium, there are some things that must not change.

First, the message of salvation must remain and take priority. If the message changes then what is the point? The Christian message is what sets it apart from all other religions. The Person of Christ, His vicarious death for the sins of all, redemption by faith, the Second Coming and the flawlessness of the Scriptures are just a few of the things that cannot change.

Second, the purpose of the Church cannot change. All those involved in the Lord's work should read Rick Warren's book, *The Purpose Driven Church.* Many churches that are still sound doctrinally have forgotten their purpose. They are content to build buildings, count heads, collect offerings, and in general—deal with things that provide activities but say little about purpose. Warren states in his book that churches are driven by eight things:

- **Tradition** - We have always done it this way.
- **Personality** - What does the leader want?
- **Finances** - How much will it cost?
- **Programs** - In program driven churches all the energy is focused on maintaining and sustaining the programs of the church.
- **Buildings** - Often funds are diverted from ministries to paying the mortgage. Warren built a large congregation before he built buildings. The reason, because he wanted to focus on people.

- **Events** - A church may have events every night without having a clear purpose for why it exists.
- **Seekers** - The church's purpose does include evangelism but not to the exclusion of all other purposes.
- **The Purpose Driven Church** - Pastor Warren points out that nothing precedes purpose:

> The starting point for every church should be this question, Why do we exist? Until you know what your church exists for, you have no foundation, no motivation and no direction for the ministry. If you are helping a new church get started, your first task is to *define* your purpose. It's far easier to set the right foundation at the start of a new church than it is to reset it after a church has existed for years.
>
> However, if you serve as pastor in an existing church that has reached a plateau, is declining or is simply discouraged—your most important task is to redefine your purpose. Forget everything else until you have established the purpose of your church in the minds of your members.
>
> Recapture a clear vision of what God wants to do in and through your church family. Absolutely nothing will revitalize a discouraged church faster than rediscovering its purpose. That purpose should encompass evangelization, discipling, nurturing and the motivation to minister to those who are being discipled.

We cannot change the fundamentals or purpose of our faith. Let's look at paradigm shifts that must be dealt with in order to minister to today's generation. Recently, while speaking to a group of pastors in California, I pointed out that many of us tend to take to heart the country song, "Lost in the Fifties Tonight." While that may have been a popular country song, it should not be the theme song of our churches. We cannot do it just like we did it in the 1950s or even the 1960s. This is a new generation with new needs and new attitudes. I have already pointed out that the message must never change, but that does not preclude changes in our methodology.

Recently I drove from Shreveport, Louisiana to Houston, Texas—cutting across East Texas. Along the way, I passed several small churches that were built fifty to seventy-five years ago. When they were built there were probably no more than a dozen homes in their immediate vacinity. Now they are surrounded by thousands of homes, with perhaps a Wal-Mart, a McDonalds and other businesses. Yet the churches have remained the same. They have failed to adapt and have also failed their communities.

One of the dilemmas the Church faces today is how to minister to new groups of young professionals. Many do not relate to the traditional church service. While I may not like that attitude, I am also not ready to write those people off as a lost generation. Although it may be more comfortable to simply minister to our older members who like things as they are, the purpose-driven ministry will attempt to find ways to minister to others as well. A plan of action may require holding services at non-traditional hours, and/or changing our messages to things that are topical to younger generations.

One of our students at LBU came to me and discussed a call he had received from a small church that had less than ten people in regular attendance. He was asked to come work as an interim pastor. I encouraged him to go. I reasoned that while he continued his studies, he could also polish his preaching skills and at the same time be a blessing to the church. Through his leadership, the church rapidly grew to eighty in attendance.

The irony is that instead of being thrilled to see a dying church revitalized, most of the original ten congregants left—citing too many changes. When speaking about change, it is always a matter of opinion as to how far change should go. I am using the illustration with that particular church only to point out that change is seldom easy.

Another pressing challenge is the prevalence of single parent families. I have spoken many times with single moms who say, "My church has no idea of what I am going through." With more than fifty percent of all marriages ending in divorce, this is a problem that is only going to grow. The First Baptist Church of Concord located in Knoxville, Tennessee, began a class for single parents. In about two months the class grew so fast that the classrooms had to be changed three times. This came about because there was a need that had to be addressed. By seeking out and meeting the needs of that church's community, the church grew from an attendance of around 700 to 3,000 people in just ten years.

A third factor will be the challenge of ever-increasing diversity. There is an explosion in the diversity of culture, of attitudes and technology. One recent study predicted that in the future, thirty percent of all Christians would abandon their local churches to worship on the Internet. While I applaud individuals who have successfully used the Internet to spread the gospel, I hope that what is reported in that study will not happen. Nothing should replace the local church. On the other hand, we have to ask ourselves, "How are we going to cope with the changes?" Frankly, I don't know the answers but I do know we need to be seeking solutions. We cannot afford to stick our heads in the sand like ostriches and hope the danger will go away.

Scripture tells us, "I will build my church; and the gates of hell shall not prevail against it" (Matthew 16:18). And, "Unto him be glory in the church by Christ Jesus throughout all ages, world without end" (Ephesians 3:21).

I have confidence that we will, with God's help, find the right methods to implement our goals for God's greatest glory. Many times in past history, the Church has faced fearful times and has always survived. Christ will protect His Bride, but that does not diminish or negate our responsibility. The Church has adapted to changes in the past, and will continue to do so in the future.

Each week I speak by phone to about twenty to thirty pastors all over America. Certainly, many of them pastor churches that are struggling, but virtually every week I also hear from churches that are experiencing outstanding growth. There *are* churches, that while holding fast to their beliefs and primary purpose, are not afraid to launch out and try new things.

In 1991, Louisiana Baptist University had far less than one-hundred active students. We began to study some of the most successful schools in America, both secular and religious. We found many things that we could adopt to our program while still holding on to our fundamentalist beliefs. We completely rebuilt our operation. Over a three-year span of time as money became available we spent three-hundred-thousand dollars rewriting our curriculum, upgrading our catalog and printing color handouts. When possible, we computerized our delivery system and all records, thereby, maximizing the output from our small staff.

Whenever possible, we designed our tests so that they could be graded electronically.

We also began to ask our students to evaluate their programs and give suggestions on how they could be improved. Through telephone surveys and written questionnaires we were able to determine and address specific needs of our curriculum. The results were nothing short of amazing. The university grew from a few students to almost 900 in just six years. Louisiana Baptist University now has over 1,300 students in over forty countries. Today, virtually all correspondence is done electronically instead of on paper.

The university has embraced change. Louisiana Baptist University is just one small example of what can happen to any school, church or business willing to adjust their paradigms to meet the ever-changing needs of their organization, while also maintaining their primary purpose and fundamental beliefs.

In Summary

Much of this chapter has been a repeat of my book, *Ten Principles of Success*. Since it was written, I have delivered numerous speeches and messages on leadership and change—both here in the U.S. and in several foreign countries. I would like to include a few of my notes from it as an addition to the "In Summary" of this chapter:

Why We Resist Change

I believe there are four basic reasons why we either do not change or resist change. One, it violates Scripture. Two, it changes our message. Three, it forces us out of our comfort zones. Four, we simply do not like change. Let's examine all four basic reasons why we resist change:

- It violates Scripture. This is a very valid reason. God's Word is always true and is not subject to the time or the whims of Man. We can never subtract from or add to the Word of God. It is always timely and up to date. It is the same yesterday, today and forever.
- It changes our message. Again, a valid reason why not to change. The gospel is still, and always will be the power of God unto salvation. I have become more and more alarmed at the current trends in the central message of many churches. The message has always been about the death, burial and resurrection of Christ. Faith and repentance are still and always will be the only means of salvation.
- Today, I hear more and more about prosperity preaching and less about Christ's blood atonement. In a conversation with Dr. John Rawlings he made this statement, "We have gotten away from an evangelistic base in our preaching. Yes, we did discipleship and counseling and all those other things but it always rested on a base of evangelism."
- It forces us out of our comfort zones. Old traditions are like an old pair of shoes—they are comfortable. New ideas and changes tend to pinch a little. Change can make us feel uncomfortable. Many traditions are good and should be respected, but we should never resist change just because it pushes us out of our personal comfort zones.
- We just don't like change. "This is the way my father did it and his father before him." Fine, go sell your car

and invest in a good horse and buggy. Disconnect your electricity and get rid of your TV. If your resistance to change only affects you, then fine, that is your right. But when it affects the Lord's work, then personal preferences must be laid aside. This is not your grandfather's day and you must deal with today's problems and challenges.

When Should Change Take Place?

- Change should take place when it is well thought out. Don't come up with a new idea or whim and immediately start implementing it. Think it through, pray about it, talk to others and only when you are convinced that it is of God, then begin to move forward.
- Change should take place when it is well-planned. Many good ideas die because of inadequate planning. Many times leaders cause great havoc when they hear a riveting speech or message at a conference; they return home inspired to change everything without carefully planning how. The end result is chaos.
- Change should come in small increments. Change is uncomfortable at best. When change is too rapid, the results are usually negative. After you have laid out a good plan you should also establish a reasonable timeline for those changes. That timeline could stretch out over several years. Always without exception, take the time to build consensus.

Always be quick to praise and slow to criticize. Create an atmosphere of mutual respect and trust. It will do wonders for the church or institution which you lead.

Chapter Six

Leaders Prioritize Their Day

Redeeming the time, because the days are evil.
—Ephesians 5:16

For a number of years, I lectured on how to put two extra hours into every day. It was called, "The 26 Hour Day." In the message I pointed out how we waste a certain amount of time every day, but with just a little planning and forethought—that time could be put into effective use. One example is to always take a book with you to the doctor's office, so you will not be sitting in the waiting room reading a three-year-old magazine—about a subject that may not be beneficial to you.

Because I put this principle to work, I was hired for a job I was seeking. I had made it a habit to always carry a notebook. While waiting for an interview, I would use that time to make notes. During one particular interview, the interviewer for the company who was hiring asked me what was I doing. When I explained that I was working so I would not lose time while waiting, he was impressed and hired me. This is just a small example of using your day wisely.

In our office at the university we work constantly. One of my pet peeves is to visit an office and see people gathered together talking, playing computer games, etc. I believe that when we work we should work without reservation, and when we play we should play joyously. I have found that combining work and play is seldom effective. In order to properly prioritize your day, you must answer the following three questions:

- How are you using your time?
- How much of it are you wasting and how are you wasting it?
- What are you going to do to stop this waste?

These are important questions and deserve earnest attention. Dr. Earl Williams, in an unpublished manuscript, categorizes people as being in one of two classes: Non-drifters and drifters. A non-drifter is a person who has a definite major purpose and a definite plan for its attainment, and is busily engaged in carrying out that plan. He thinks his own thoughts and assumes full responsibility for them, whether they are right or wrong.

A drifter does no real thinking but he accepts the thoughts, ideas and opinions of others, and acts upon them as if they were his own. The drifter follows the line of least resistance with everything and repeats his mistakes over and over again; while the non-drifter takes pride in blazing new trails, mastering new hazards and learns from his mistakes.

A non-drifter expresses action through definiteness of purpose, and he follows the habit of going the extra mile in carrying out his purpose. He moves ahead on his own personal initiative without pressure from others. He controls all of his habits, thoughts and actions—through the strictest kind of self-discipline. He maintains a positive mental attitude and thinks in terms of what he desires most, not what he does not desire. He supports his actions with applied faith.

A non-drifter surrounds himself with a mastermind group in order that he may have the cooperation of others—whose knowledge and experience he needs to carry out his purpose. He recognizes his weaknesses and finds the ways and means of bridging them. He takes personal inventory of himself as regularly as a first class merchant takes inventory of his stock. The non-drifter engages in an occupation of his own choice. Therefore he is engaged in work which truly is a labor of love, into which he willingly projects his creative ability, his enthusiasm, his hopes and his desired goals.

Drifters seldom concern themselves over the selection of an occupation suited to their education or to their mental and spiritual temperaments. Dr. Williams points out the drifter makes no attempt to discipline or control his thoughts, and never learns the difference between negative thoughts and positive thoughts. He allows his mind to be occupied with any stray thought that may float into it.

People who drift in connection with their thought habits are sure to drift when it comes to other subjects as well. A positive mental attitude cannot be attained by the drifter. It can, however, be obtained by a scrupulous regard for time through the habit of self-discipline. No amount of time devoted to one's occupation can compensate for the benefits of a positive mental attitude, for this is the underlying power of God-given wisdom that makes the use of time effective and productive.

Time Wasters

Avoid time wasters. We can always come across people who have little or nothing to do, and are looking for someone to do nothing with. If you are not careful, people like this will take large sums of time from your day and you will find yourself up late at night (doing what you should have done during the day). Because of the nature of their work, I think pastors and other religious leaders are especially susceptible to time wasters. Pastors and religious leaders must be caring and thoughtful, but unless they are careful, they will find themselves losing great portions of each day to time wasters. Wise use of time is something everyone should be mindful of in order to avoid falling into a "going nowhere" trap.

When I served as a pastor, I became aware over the years that although I served a congregation of hundreds—a handful of people (probably less than a dozen) took up most of my time. They did not need counseling or spiritual help. These people were just bored. They had nothing to do and were looking for others who did not have a schedule. They became even more engaged if they found someone who was a good storyteller, and always had fresh coffee available. In my case, to remedy the problem of time wasters overstaying their welcome, I began to develop different techniques to close out conversations and get back to work. At times, my secretary, having been previously alerted—would come into my office to remind me of some task or appointment. And sometimes I would simply pick up some tracts and say, "Since you are not busy would you mind making some visits?" Usually this would clear out the office in a hurry.

As a university president, I do not have to be quite so delicate. There is always something to do; so I have a legitimate reason to terminate the time I spend with a visitor. I have also developed a routine that usually works when necessary. After five, or at the most—ten minutes, I simply stand up, pick up some papers from my desk and extend my hand. (I explain that something must be taken care of and I am sure that my guest will understand.) I then accompany my visitor out of my office, walk to my secretary's desk and engage her in conversation. As my guest leaves our section of the office heading for the exit, I call out some pleasantry and then continue giving instructions to my secretary in order to avoid starting a fresh conversation with my departing visitor. This diplomatic approach works almost every time.

I am not saying that we should work all the time. Unless we periodically take some time off, we will face burnout and lose productivity. I *am* saying that we should plan those hours we intend to work and also schedule in time to relax. Do not fall into a haphazard lifestyle that causes you to be unproductive. Take charge, organize and be in control of your day. I have taught that we should organize our day into three categories. The following chart will help you develop and plan your day. After many years, I do not always use the chart itself but I always use the principle. As I drive to work each morning, I rehearse in my mind those things that must absolutely be completed. They then take top priority.

If you are not careful you will be operating out of column three instead of column one. When you do follow column three first, then you will be eating a long lunch with your friends while the check you wrote for the light bill bounces and your utility service is disconnected. Not to mention that instead of eating a home cooked meal that evening with the groceries you were supposed to buy, you are calling Domino's late at night when the kids need to be in bed.

TODAY

MUST BE DONE	NEED TO DO	LIKE TO DO
Make bank deposit.	Wash the car.	Have lunch with friends.
Pay bills.	Buy groceries (depends on how low you are).	Play golf with buddies.
Do laundry.	Clean the house.	Go shopping.
Mow the lawn.	Plan meals for the week.	Watch TV.

TOMORROW

MUST BE DONE	NEED TO DO	LIKE TO DO

NEXT WEEK

MUST BE DONE	NEED TO DO	LIKE TO DO

Being Too Busy

Most of us spend our lives working. The question is this: What type of work and how long are we working each day? A vast amount of our time is spent on activities and things (busyness) that are virtually unnecessary, both personally and professionally. The logical conclusion to change those dynamics would be to work smarter not harder. The problem with this common sense idea is this: It is easier said than done!

We have created habits and mindsets and often think unless we are rushing to or from something, we think we are wasting time. The trick is to break that habit. I have discovered that many times the busyness I have created, is really an unproductive use of time in disguise. The first step to correcting busyness is to focus on the critical few—rather than the insignificant many. Jack Miller, president of the Quill Corporation, makes these excellent points:

> There are many, many things that we do in our business (as well as personal) lives that simply don't make much difference. With most of these, even if you do them extremely well, they won't "move the needle" at all.
>
> You won't notice any difference in the bottom line profit or in your paycheck. And that's bad enough. But what is really worse is that when you are so busy doing all those things, you don't really have enough time (or energy) to do a really good job on those "critical few" items that, if properly implemented, can bring great results.
>
> It is important to realize that there are two levels of what is "insignificant" and what is "critical." At the first level is the question of whether the activity is totally insignificant to the success of the company. If it is, it shouldn't be done – at all – by anyone. The second level is the question of whether the activity is something that should be done, but, perhaps, by someone else in the organization.

Having been an employer for over 40 years, I have observed that there are some that are always busy but actually produce very little. This is brought about by poor planning, faulty execution, and improper use of our time. Dr. George Flanagan, corporate psychologist and lecturer, points out that we often confuse activity for accomplishment.

Time is a valuable commodity that once it is spent can never be recovered. Well spoken is the sign that stated: "What I do today is important because I am paying a day of my life for it. What I accomplish must be worthwhile because the price is high."

In Summary

A day is a precious thing; it should not be wasted or squandered. I don't mind working hard but I do despise a day when I have worked hard all day and have accomplished nothing. We all have those days but through proper planning and execution we can minimize them. Plan your tasks and schedule them in sequence so your day doesn't turn into a helter-skelter mess.

When I was still active as a pastor in Cincinnati, Ohio, which is a fairly large city, hospital visits were a part of my schedule every week. Hospitals are scattered over all parts of the city. I soon developed the most efficient route to visit all the hospitals that housed any of our church members.

I would then allow just so many minutes for each stop. This would make it possible to take care of all my visits in about one half day. Obviously, if an emergency occurred I would adjust my plans, but in most cases by planning ahead I could save several hours each week and still meet all my commitments.

Time is precious. Once it is gone we can never get it back. Use every day in a positive way, achieving positive results. This will also give you more free time to spend with family and loved ones.

Chapter Seven

Prioritize Your Life

First seek ye the kingdom of God and those things shall be added unto you.
—Matthew 6:33

Everyone should have a clear priority list. If you do not have your priorities written down you should have them distinctly memorized. What are the things that are most important in your life? It is easy to give the stock answer but are we being honest? Honest with others and with ourselves? The person that you need to be most truthful with is yourself. Shakespeare wrote, "To thine own self be true." Sometimes we need to stop and check our goals, motivations, tactics and attitudes. I believe a very simple priority list should be something like this:

- God
- Family
- Church

- Others
- Self
- Satisfying Career
- Money

Most people would move up the last entry on the list. I do not intend to minimize the importance of money. One fellow said, "I have had money and I have been without money, and I can tell you that having money is more convenient." All of us could say "Amen" to that. It certainly makes life easier if we can have a comfortable home, a dependable car and all the food and clothing we need. It is a feeling of great comfort to know that you can pay your bills and still have some left over for the so-called "rainy day."

God, of course, should be number one on your priority list. Earlier in this book I stated that there is nothing particularly spiritual about poverty. One of the first jokes I learned as a young pastor went something like this:

> As the church knelt around the altar for chain prayer, the minister, in deep sincerity prayed, "Lord keep me humble, even if you have to keep me poor, keep me humble." With equal sincerity, the deacon next to him prayed, "Lord keep our minister humble. You keep him humble and we will keep him poor."

Some people seem to equate poverty with spirituality. A careful study of Scripture reveals that those who were used by God had various backgrounds and financial circumstances. Paul scarcely had enough money to sustain himself. But on the other hand, Abraham, David and Solomon were wealthy men. We might point to the fact that wealth corrupted Solomon but most of that wealth was accumulated while he was in fellowship with God. I believe that the Bible teaches us the very characteristics and work ethics that tend to make us successful.

"Commit your works to the LORD and your plans will be established" (Proverbs 16:3).

I believe that God intends for us to prosper—not in some miraculous way but because we have followed His principles throughout our lives. However, again, I point out that success is more than wealth. In fact, history has proven that some of the most miserable people were also the wealthiest. The world's wealthiest people also have the highest rate of alcoholism and suicide. Scripture admonishes us that we are to put God first in our lives.

We should always seek His will first. In a message I heard over thirty-five years ago, Dr. Jerry Falwell stated, "Man's greatest responsibility is to find God's will and do it." If we always put God first in our lives it will help us to keep all other things in perspective.

When I worked actively as a pastor, I remember the times when missionary families were guests of our family. We always tried to do well by them, housing them in excellent hotels and taking them to some of our favorite restaurants. They were always appropriately appreciative, but would often remark about how they were homesick.

The remarkable thing was that the home they missed was a hut somewhere along a river in Africa; a home with no air conditioning; little, if any, refrigeration and electricity and very few of what we call "creature comforts." Why would these missionaries be homesick for such a primitive lifestyle? Because it was God's will for their lives to be there and God's will is our place of true peace, refuge and comfort.

I remember that as a 21-year-old seminary student, I held a short revival meeting in Portage, Missouri. The little church building was perched on the levy of the Mississippi River. Next to the church was a small farmhouse that served as a parsonage. Each night the family and I would gather around the table for a simple meal prepared from vegetables and fruits that had been raised in the garden. We would hold hands as we gathered around the table.

Each child from the oldest to the youngest would say grace thanking God for all He had provided. In the grand scheme of things this young family may seem insignificant but they are not; they were living in the will of God every day. We can do no more important work than what God has called us to do. All this took place over fifty years ago but there was so much love and joy in that little house that I have never forgotten that special week.

Second on your list should be family.

So many times in life I have met people who said something to this effect: I have been a tremendous professional success. I have set high goals for myself and met or exceeded all of them. I am at the top of my profession. I am a financial success; I have an expensive car, a big house and a large bank account. But I am miserable because I lost my family. I don't feel like I even know my wife/husband and children anymore and I find that all those things that I thought were so important are no longer satisfying.

In 1972, George McGovern was running for president against Richard Nixon. Later in life, he wrote a book about his daughter, Keri, who was an alcoholic. They found her frozen to death in a drunken stupor in 1994. At that time, George McGovern was still spending eighteen hours a day working for political causes.

While reading his daughter's diary he found that he hadn't been the parent he thought he had been. While spending time as a politician, Keri was writing in her diary about how much she missed her daddy and that he probably didn't really care about her.

In his book, *Terry: My daughter's Life-and-Death Struggle with Alcoholism*, George McGovern emphasized the need for parents to spend time with their kids, especially teenagers. This would ensure that neither the parents or children will ever have regrets that they were too busy for one another. George McGovern said, "I'd give everything I have…I mean everything…to spend one more afternoon with Keri, to let her know how much I love her."

Without a doubt we live in a very disturbing time. There has never been a more difficult time for the family. Even when we do our best it is difficult. If we have family time ranked low on our priority list, then we are doomed to fail.

Third, I must emphasize the importance of the local church in our lives.

We are admonished in Scripture to not forsake the assembling of ourselves together. In Ephesians 3:21 we are told "unto Him be glory in the church..." The church is not only important because it is a place of preaching and edification, but because it surrounds us with the right kind of friends.

It has been repeatedly proven that to some extent, we are all influenced by the company we keep. Our involvement with a local church gives us an opportunity to not only feed on the Word of God, but to develop a system of friends that can have a positive influence on our lives.

I have placed "others" fourth on the priority list for a number of reasons.

First, I believe that it is a principle taught in Scripture. Second, I believe that when we begin to center all our attention on ourselves, we have a tendency to become more selfish, covetous, jealous, paranoid and just generally maladjusted. When we place the emphasis on others, we feel a sense of satisfaction when they succeed.

After God, family, church and others we place ourselves, then our careers.

It is appropriate to separate those two categories because I do not think that we should be defined simply by our careers. We should all try to build some time into our schedules for ourselves. As I mentioned earlier, even Christ, at times would come apart from the crowds.

There are times that we do need to stop and smell the roses. This is not depriving those that we love of anything. It is simply acknowledging the fact that after personal relaxation we can be a better person for those with whom we interact.

Finally, we will list career and money respectively.
A career should, in some way, be rewarding and satisfying in more ways than just proving an income. Remember this: You spend more time at work than anywhere else. If you hate what you do, you will be miserable for most of your life. That does *not* mean you should go into work tomorrow and quit your job. It *does* mean you should begin to seek appropriate training and whatever else it takes to eventually change professions.

None of us should spend a lifetime doing something we hate. Sometimes change does not come quickly, but every day that we delay taking those first steps toward change, will mean one more day of misery. I once heard this statement, "If you want a shade tree in your back yard, the best time to plant it was twenty years ago, the second best time is now."

Many years ago when my children were very young, our family was on vacation at Daytona Beach. While my wife bathed our children and prepared them for bed, I spent a short time in the hotel's hot tub located downstairs away from our room. Only one other person was there, a gentleman from Miami. As we struck up a conversation he began to talk about his life.

He had been raised in North Carolina and studied law at one of their prestigious universities. He had entered law school with high ideals of how he could help humanity and in some way make a positive difference. He went on to describe how he had joined a large Miami law firm and began to represent high profile clients. He became a part of the so-called "in crowd."

Along the way he lost sight of his original goals and began to become involved in some cases of a questionable nature. He told me how he had become exceedingly wealthy with an oceanfront home and expensive sports car. Along the way, he ruined his marriage, alienated his children and lost his self-respect.

He shared with me that he was about to return to North Carolina to try to find the man he had once been. His first stop was to be at the small country church that he attended as a boy. As we bowed our heads in prayer, we both shed some tears. His story is tragic, but not unusual.

A question we might ask is this: "Who is truly a rich man?" In the Gospel of Luke, chapter 12, verses 15-21, notice closely, for these are the words of Jesus Christ Himself:

> "And He said unto them, take heed, and beware of covetousness; for a man's life consisteth not in the abundance of things which he possesseth. And He spake a parable unto them saying, [a parable is truth illustrated in human life] "the ground of a certain rich man brought forth plentifully."
>
> And he thought within himself, saying, [now watch the wording closely] what shall I do, because I have no room where to bestow my fruits? And he said, this will I do; I

> will pull down my barns and build greater, and there will I bestow [warehouse] all my fruits and my goods.
>
> But God said unto him, 'Thou fool, this night thy soul shall be required of thee: then whose shall those things be, which thou hast provided? So is he that layeth up treasure for himself, and is not rich toward God.'"

Here is a description of a man who had a serious disease, which is sometimes called too much Me, Myself and I…too much self. Self is the center of his world. Self is his god. Everything he owns is "mine." He continues to say, "And I will say to my soul, thou hast much goods laid up for many years; take thine ease; eat, drink and be merry." He reasons within himself that he has plenty; that he can retire early, enjoy himself and "live it up."

Verse 20 is a startling contrast: "But God said unto him, 'Thou fool. This night thy soul shall be required of thee.'" Not his material wealth, but his soul. He has failed miserably in his stewardship of life; now he must answer to God. We are all answerable individually to God. Then we read, "Whose shall those things be, which thou has provided?" Now look at verse 21: "So is he that layeth up treasure for himself and is not rich toward God."

Are we rich toward God? Or as with this man in the parable, are we pouring out our lives to build a temporal estate—earthly treasures that perish? Are we constantly working in order to buy a bigger house, to have more automobiles, to have more stocks and bonds, to have more affluence and influence in society, to exercise more power over people to feed our pride and ego?

The truly rich man is the man who has successfully accomplished the first six priorities listed in this chapter: God, family, church, others, self and a satisfying career. If he has accomplished these things, there is also a good chance that he will also be financially successful because these six things are the building blocks to success.

Remember that it is not money but the *love* of money that is the root of all evil. I have at least two or three friends who are millionaires and yet have a humble servant's heart. They are faithful Christians who have not lost sight of the really valuable things in life.

Pay careful attention to the teaching of the Lord Jesus Christ in the Gospel of Matthew, chapter 6 verses 25-33:

> "Therefore I say unto you, Take no thought for your life, what ye shall eat, or what ye shall drink; nor yet for your body, what ye shall put on. Is not the life more than meat, and the body than raiment?'
>
> Therefore I say unto you, Take no thought for your life, what ye shall eat, or what ye shall drink; nor yet for your body, what ye shall put on. Is not the life more than meat, and the body than raiment?
>
> Behold the fowls of the air: for they sow not, neither do they reap, nor gather into barns; yet your heavenly Father feedeth them. Are ye not much better than they?
>
> Which of you by taking thought can add one cubit unto his stature? And why take ye thought for raiment? Consider

> the lilies of the field, how they grow; they toil not, neither do they spin:
>
> And yet I say unto you, That even Solomon in all his glory was not arrayed like one of these. Wherefore, if God so clothe the grass of the field, which to day is, and to morrow is cast into the oven, shall he not much more clothe you, O ye of little faith?
>
> Therefore take no thought, saying, What shall we eat? or, what shall we drink? Or, wherewithal shall we be clothed? (For after all these things do the Gentiles seek:) for your heavenly Father knoweth that ye have need of all these things.
>
> But seek ye first the kingdom of God, and his righteousness; and all these things shall be added unto you."

Aren't the very things Jesus describes important to us? Yes, but Jesus says that we should not be obsessed with them. Life is more than eating. Life is more than wearing clothing. There is a much deeper, broader, more eternal purpose in life which the Lord Jesus Christ is teaching us about in this passage. We see the conclusion in Matthew 6:33, where God admonishes us to seek Him first: "But seek ye first the kingdom of God and His righteousness, and all these things shall be added unto you."

Notice the Lord Jesus says ALL (life sustaining things) will be added unto you. God is our greatest Advocate and He wants what is best for us. Living in His will, living by His precepts every day of our lives will give us a peace that surpasses all understanding (Philippians 4:7).

> "For I know the thoughts that I think toward you, saith the LORD, thoughts of peace, and not of evil, to give you an expected end" (Jeremiah 29:11).

In Summary

This might be the time to ask the question: What are my priorities? It's easy to say, "Oh, they are the seven points mentioned earlier in this chapter." But do our actions testify to our words? Ever since God called me into the ministry at the young age of twenty, His will for my life has certainly been a priority. I have had a good ministry. But now, over forty years later, I look back and see that I could have done so much more.

I think I have been a pretty good dad to my two children. I attended all of their ballgames and tried to be there for all of their important occasions. We remain very close; but they both live in distant states. We only get to spend a few days together each year. I look back and wish I would have had more fishing trips with my son and more special daddy and daughter afternoons.

Determine what has priority in your life and then live up to those priorities. One of the saddest things in life is to look back and realize that our God-given opportunities were squandered.

Chapter Eight

Leaders Are Willing to Do the Hard Things

Except the Lord build the house, they labour in vain that build it: except the Lord keep the city, the watchman waketh but in vain. —*Psalm 127:1*

I almost titled this chapter, "Eat the Spinach First." As a child I developed a habit of always eating first, the item on my plate I liked the least. It could be spinach, Brussels sprouts or liver. In those days you did not come to the table and pick and choose what you would like to eat. You were required to consume everything on your plate. Because I did not want to end the meal with the taste of spinach or liver in my mouth, I would always eat those items first, so I could enjoy the rest of the food.

I have found that prioritizing things that same way is a good philosophy for life. It is our nature to gravitate toward tasks that interest us the most, things that are the easiest to manage—or give us instant gratification. We tend to deal with the hard problems last. I have found when we don't deal with the things which we consider harder, distasteful or undesirable, they escalate into bigger problems. The sooner we deal with the more challenging issues, the better. This is true at any level but especially for those who hold leadership positions. As a leader, you know how to deal with the bigger, harder problems. That is the reason why you have a large salary, perhaps a large office, and company benefits that far exceed those of the other employees.

When difficult problems arise, remember the reason you get paid what you are paid is because of your ability to deal with and solve problems. If there were no problems, then there would be no need for problem solvers; and as a leader you would probably be out of a job. Rather than feel sorry for yourself, look at it as a challenge that causes you to grow both intellectually and spiritually. When I was younger, I had a great tendency to procrastinate. Many times I sought a stop gap or temporary solution, rather than deal directly with a problem. I look back at many instances where my failure to act in a timely fashion, later brought even bigger problems.

Most of us have a desire to ignore problems hoping they will work themselves out. But that seldom happens. Disregarded problems can quickly take on the nature of pesky weeds—growing deeper roots, which eventually require more drastic action to eradicate them. When a problem arises it requires a tentative decision and then action. First, we must make an informed decision. Making an informed decision requires that we study all available data, and counsel with those that can give us quality advice. If we have a desire to do so, we can usually find important knowledge and carefully crafted advice from a variety of sources.

Once we have gathered and explored information to help resolve a problem, we can then make a qualified decision. But we must have the c*ourage* to act. I emphasize the word, "courage." Throughout our lives we are constantly called upon to make decisions and take actions that we would rather avoid. One of the hardest things I have had to come to grips with as a leader was firing people that I personally liked, but were a liability to the organization. This is especially true when replacing church personnel. In the case of church personnel, a leader not only has to deal with the unpleasant task of firing someone, but the potential reaction (negative or positive) of the congregation.

I have found that once you are convinced that someone must be dismissed, action needs to be taken immediately. When you make the move, do it diplomatically but firmly. While it remains an unpleasant task, I have taught myself that this is simply another function of management, another task that must be preformed. When you have made a decision, take responsibility for it. I have always appreciated people who are willing to take responsibility for their actions.

I am too young to remember much of Harry Truman's presidency, but one thing I have always appreciated is his reputation for being willing to accept responsibility. He coined the phrase, "The buck stops here." Good or bad, agree or not agree—he never tried to shift responsibility or shift blame. Truman had several difficult decisions that marked his presidency. First, was the dropping of the first atomic bomb. Probably no other president ever faced a tougher decision. To drop the bomb would mean death to hundreds of thousands of civilians. A second tough decision was the firing of Douglas McArthur. General McArthur was a national hero revered by many Americans. In many circles he was far more popular than the president. People still debate the wisdom of that decision, but not Truman's courage to make the decision.

Bill Clinton displayed some talent, charisma and intelligence during his presidency. He had great ability and in the opinion of most people, he will go down in history as a good president. Through a careless act of adultery, he soiled the presidency and left a blot on his personal legacy. While this saddened many Americans, I believe that they were even more disappointed that he lied to the American people—that he was unwilling to accept responsibility for his actions. Many people that formerly supported him had a great problem with the fact that for seven months he cowered in the White House while he sent his wife and his staff out to lie to the press.

When David committed adultery with Bathsheba and then had her husband killed, he probably thought he had put the problem to rest. Then God sent the prophet Nathan to say, "Thou art the man." Even if one disagrees with the tactics of the prosecutor, even if as Hillary said, "There is a vast rightwing conspiracy," Bill Clinton still had to face the fact that he was "the man." That it was he who committed salacious acts an lied, and it was he and no one else who had to take responsibility—full responsibility.

We must all at times take full responsibility for unpleasant decisions, and at times—for glaring mistakes. There is a simple formula. It is this: BE—DO—HAVE. The BE part simply means that you must first be a person of integrity and character. Many times people have risen to power by projecting a false image of themselves. Any success that they might have is usually short-lived because their true nature surfaces. God can and does bless character. Character is more important than talent, personality or beauty.

Second, we must DO. Occasionally someone will become successful by what seems to be pure luck. However, most successful people prevail because they have good work ethics and unwavering determination. They are the people who are doers, not talkers. Many people are great dreamers and talk a lot about what they intend to do. However, most of their dreams never come true because they fail to take the necessary steps to succeed.

I once heard a simple little story that made such an impression on me that I have told it many times when giving lectures. It seems that a young couple had been looking for a special keepsake for a memorable event in their lives. In search of this special object, they visited an antique shop.

On the very top shelf the couple spotted a tiny teapot. Taking it down, they marveled at the intricate little object and said, "This is the most beautiful teapot in the world." The teapot spoke back to them and said, "I was not always a beautiful teapot. I was once a gray lump of clay. The master potter scooped me up and began to pound and roll me in his hand. He pounded and rolled, pounded and rolled and I cried, 'Master please stop.' He simply answered, 'I am not finished yet.' Then he placed me on the potter's wheel and it began to turn."

"Again I cried, 'Stop, please stop!' Again he answered, 'I am not finished yet.' Then he placed me in a hot oven. Again I cried, 'Stop, please stop!' Again he replied, 'I am not finished yet.' Then he removed me and began to paint me. Then, again, he placed me in the oven as I cried, 'Please stop.' Again his answer came, 'I am not finished yet.' So you see, it is not easy to be a beautiful teapot. It took a lot of sacrifice and pain on my part."

May we all be as aware as that teapot and accept all that the Master may use to make us a beautiful and useful vessel ready for service. We are admonished in Scripture that we will succeed if we faint not (Galatians 6:9). We will HAVE, if we are willing first to BE and then DO. We shall eventually have those things that will equip us for even greater service. Success may not happen as quickly as we like, but it will happen if you have character and a good work ethic. Some of the world's greatest successes have failed several times but there was something within them that drove them to bounce back and try again.

In Summary

All leaders must, at times make difficult decisions. As a pastor, I had to preach sermons that I did not want to preach. But problems arise and it is the pastor's responsibility to take care of them. Sometimes as a university president, I have to make decisions that I would rather ignore or put off. But I cannot, because it is my responsibility to do what is best for LBU.

When hard decisions must be made, we must pray for wisdom and guidance. I have often in my life had to go to the prayer closet, and at times in tears, seek God's will; and also His plan as to how I should deal with an existing situation. When hard decisions must be made, they should only be made after much thought, careful planning and much fervent prayer.

Leaders Associate with Others Who Will Help Them Grow

A wise man will hear, and will increase learning; and a man of understanding shall attain unto wise counsels.
—Proverbs 1:15

When I was 27 years old I visited Dr. John Rawlings, pastor of Landmark Baptist Church. At that time, Landmark's weekly Sunday School attendance was 4,500. It was a great honor to meet this man who had accomplished so much. His advice to me was this: "Son, always run with a crowd that is a little better than you are, and you will always continue to grow."

Dr. Rawlings went on to explain how so many pastors, after they have obtained only limited success, will form their own associations or fellowships. Into their organizations the pastors will attract a group of men who have had a lesser amount of success. Thereby, the pastor will become the self-appointed leader of the group—the proverbial big fish in a little pond. Because he is already the leader, he feels little or no need to challenge himself and continue to grow. Had that pastor methodically sought out those who were more successful, who knew more, who were growing—he would have grown as well.

It is especially easy for a pastor, teacher, counselor or businessperson to go through a learning process for a few years, reach a certain comfort level and stay there for the rest of their lives. I have met many preachers who are still preaching at the same level they were ten or fifteen years ago. They fall back on what they already know, and do not seek out fresh messages for their flock.

Many teachers teach the same courses year after year. In a dull monotone they recite endless facts and then wonder why their students are uninspired. Counselors give the same routine advice over and over, without spending the time or energy to really meet the individual needs of their clients. Business people who refuse to change and grow are usually eliminated, or stagnate in some lower level job that offers little opportunity to advance.

We should never accept mediocrity. We must continue to grow. Make it a point to follow after people who are successful. Watch what they do. Ask them questions. Read books. Watch videos. Listen to audio tapes. Subscribe to magazines. In general, do all you can to better equip yourself to actualize all of your God-given potential.

In high school, I had a science teacher named Lynn Sasser. Mr. Sasser was a teacher who cared a great deal about his students. Along with science, he would often give us a lesson about life. I remember he brought a very ripe red tomato to one of his classes. Holding up the tomato to the class he said, "Let me give you some advice. You see this beautiful ripe tomato? In a few days it will be rotten because the next step after ripe is rotten." He went on to admonish us to always be green and growing. I have never forgotten that, and I determined on that day that I would never get ripe; that I would always continue to learn new things and grow.

One of the greatest pianists I have ever personally met is Dr. Charles Novell. What he can do on a piano is nothing short of amazing. He still practices daily. Each week he sits at his piano for dozens of hours practicing scales and learning new improvisations. I once asked him, "Why?" He replied, "I don't want to slip, and besides that, I am still learning."

We must choose a life of growth. The only way to improve the quality of our lives is to continue to improve ourselves. I was recently discussing competition with a couple of my staff members. I explained that when I was younger I was in competition with others. Somewhere along the way I switched the target from others to myself.

I now have only one person I am in competition with—me. I am in constant competition to be a better me…a little smarter, a little more efficient and a little more productive. I study harder than ever. I often say, "You *can* teach an old dog new tricks and I am living proof."

After twenty-five years as a pastor, I shifted gears and became a college president. I will not pretend that I was a complete novice when I arrived at LBU. But several books could be written about what I did not know about running a university. I immediately set out to learn. I used the same formula I had used all throughout my life. I set out to find those who were better and more experienced. I visited several outstanding schools. I reviewed files and asked questions—lots of questions. I feel that through those actions I moved LBU ahead by at least five years.

John Maxwell, in his book, *Breakthrough Parenting*, points out that you are only young once but you can be immature forever. That's because growth is not automatic. Just because you grow older doesn't mean you keep on growing. Maxwell, in his book, *The Success Journey: The Process of Living Your Dreams*, has a section on being teachable. In it he cites the case of John Wooden. Former UCLA basketball coach, John Wooden, is an inspiring model of personal growth. He continually developed himself. He did the same with his players—trying to help them reach greater heights of excellence and success.

One of my favorite sayings from his book is this, "It's what you learn after you know it all that counts." Wooden recognized that the greatest obstacle to growth isn't ignorance, it's knowledge. The more you learn, the greater the chance you will think you know it all. And if that happens, you become unteachable and you are no longer growing—or improving.

John Wooden continued to learn and grow, even while he was at the top of his profession. For example, after he had already won a national championship (an accomplishment that most college coaches never achieve, he scrapped the offense he had used for years). Instead, he learned a completely new offense in order to maximize the potential of his team as well as the talents of one player—Lewis Alcindor (now known as Kareem Abdul-Jabbar. The result was awe-inspiring. John Wooden and his teams moved to an even higher level of play and won additional consecutive national championships. If you are to reach your potential, you have to keep growing just as John Wooden did. When you remain teachable, your potential is almost limitless.

While still in my twenties, I preached a revival at a church in Georgetown, Delaware. The pastor had also arranged for me to do a one-hour talk show each day on the radio. People would call in and ask me any question they chose. I had no idea what the questions might be. It was a difficult task to say the least. I told the pastor that if he ever got another idea like that for the next revival—not to call me. Nevertheless, each day I sat before an open mike and answered questions such as, "Where did Cain get his wife and who are the two witnesses in Revelation?"

One day I received a very provocative question from a caller: "When did you preach your worst sermon?" I thought for a moment, took the question into the present tense and answered, "Right after I preach my best sermon." The reason being, that right after we begin to feel that we have arrived and begin to feel our greatness, God has to pull us back down to earth and show us just how fallible we are.

God has blessed me greatly. I have traveled to many foreign countries and have preached in some of the world's greatest churches. That is more than a boy from a small town in southern Kentucky ever had a right to expect; and I want to keep it that way. If I ever get to the place where I expect privileges or even think that I deserve them, then life will cease to be fun, and it will stop my growth.

I want to continue to be amazed at what God can do. I want to continue to be a little nervous when I get up before a crowd. Large or small, I want to continue to worry about, "Will I do my best on this occasion?" After fifty years in the pulpit and after thousands of sermons, it would be easy to fall back on what I learned and become complacent.

When I was a young preacher, an older pastor commented on a sermon I had just preached. He stated that when he was young he had also paced and shouted when he preached. He went on to say that after a few years, I would "settle down." I prayed that night, "Lord never let me settle down." Many times we fall into a comfort zone. We have accomplished enough to be comfortable. We are no longer challenged.

The great preacher R.G. Lee was known for his sermon, "Payday Someday." Another one of his sermons that had a more profound effect on me was the message titled, "The Menace of Mediocrity." In that message he speaks of the tragedy of those who are able to soar as eagles tweeting as sparrows, those with steam shovel capacity digging in the dirt with a teaspoon and those capable of playing in the symphony blowing tunes on a plastic flute. In his book, *Success Journey*, John Maxwell states:

> A factor in your personal development comes in the area of your relationships with others. Carefully examine your closest associations. You can tell a lot about which direction your life is heading by looking at the people with whom you have chosen to spend your time and share your ideas. Their values and priorities affect the way you think and act. If they're positive people dedicated to growth, then their values and priorities will encourage you and reinforce your desire to develop yourself.

Taking Dr. Rawling's admonition to heart to run with those a little better than me, has given me the chance to rub shoulders with some of God's greatest. From those great preachers, educators and businessmen, I have learned lessons that have allowed me to grow, and I continue to surround myself with intelligent, dedicated people. Through their encouragement and guidance, I have been able to also have a measure of success. If you dedicate yourself to personal growth, there is no telling where it will take you; and you can rest assured that it will always be up.

In the mid-eighties, I was very involved in the gospel music industry. As president of the Gospel Music Network, we produced shows heard on 120 radio stations in twenty states. In that position, I often visited Nashville, Tennessee. I happened to visit the office of the recording company that produced Garth Brooks' first hit. There were banners and signs everywhere advertising the fact that Garth's song was number one in the nation. Garth went on to produce many hit records and became one of the most recognized artists in the world.

At a concert in Central Park in New York, Garth Brooks drew a crowd that was estimated at a quarter of a million people. It was not always that way. The first time Garth went to Nashville he was a failure. He even gave up and returned home. But there burned within him a flame that would not let him give-up. He returned to Nashville and the rest is history.

Growth is a choice that we must choose. It doesn't come upon us by accident. Conscious effort must be made and a price must be paid. Making the choice to grow and continue growing does not guarantee that we will be rich and famous or be cited in the history books. It does guarantee that we will be better people than if we never made the choice.

In Summary

I have always been blessed to have an outstanding circle of friends and acquaintances. One of my first contacts in the ministry was Dr. I. K. Cross. He was president of the seminary I attended. I was blessed to travel and speak in some conferences with him. I have always maintained that he is one of the two men who most influences my ministry.

The other great friend was Dr. John Rawlings. I first became acquainted with Dr. Rawlings when at the age of 27, I moved to

Cincinnati, Ohio. We soon became close friends and remained close until his death. Dr. Rawlings introduced me to such greats as B. R. Lakin, Harold Henniger and Dallas Billington. I also became friends with Tommy Trammell, who in turn introduced me to Jerry Falwell.

In my twenties I preached in conferences with R. G. Lee and became acquainted with John R. Rice. Other friends included Lee Robertson, Charles Keene and Chancellor J. G. Tharpe. Two other friendships that I cultivated were with two great Christian businessmen, Joe Lewis and Tom Rapier.

Early on I attended a school for pastors and became acquainted with Jack Hyles. I became friends with Lester Rolloff. In fact, I spoke on the phone to him the day before he died in a tragic plane crash.

All these men and many others like them inspired me. They had all accomplished so much more than I had at that point in my life, and they challenged me to do more. You can never go wrong when you surround yourself with a circle of good friends—people who know the Lord, who are full of character and are high achievers. They will have a profound influence on your life.

Chapter Ten

Leaders Set Goals

Wherefore seeing we also are compassed about with so great a cloud of witnesses, let us lay aside every weight, and the sin which doth so easily beset us, and let us run with patience the race that is set before us.
—Hebrews 12:1

Setting goals is like any other decision; they should be set only after much deliberation and assessment of opportunities. Many people are guilty of setting goals that are built more on fantasy than reality. Some people have no goals and simply drift along accepting whatever life brings. Some people set goals far beyond what they can expect to attain. Both extremes can spell disaster. Everyone should have some well-defined and established goals. They can be written or non-written. But I prefer a written list that you can refer to occasionally as both a reminder and a checklist.

> "Brethren, I count not myself to have apprehended: but this one thing I do, forgetting those things which are behind and reaching forth unto those things which are before. I press toward the mark for prize of the high calling of God in Christ Jesus." —Philippians 3:13-14

When I came to Louisiana Baptist University I spent my first weeks investigating the condition of the school, and establishing a list of goals. I have changed those goals somewhat, and of course updated them from time to time. However, most of them are fairly close to the original goals that were written in the fall of 1990. One of the things that every business student learns is how to write a business plan. I have read several definitions of what a business plan should contain. Let me share with you my simple definition; a business plan should indicate:

- Where you are.
- Where you want to be.
- How you plan to get there.

While it is important to set goals, it is just as important to set the right kind of goals. They should be realistic and have the right motives behind them. If you set goals that are inherently unattainable, then you face almost certain failure. While all of us face failure from time to time (there are lessons to be learned in failure), we should never set ourselves up to fail. With each goal, also establish what it will take to reach that goal. Be aggressive in your goals but also be reasonable. If you continually set your goals too high and constantly fail, then after a while you will become negative and cynical about yourself and others.

The first question usually associated with goal setting deals is this: "Is it right to set goals?" Paul, in Philippians 3:14 wrote, "I press toward the mark for the prize of the high calling of God in Christ Jesus." It is clear that he had some specific goals. On another occasion Paul said that one of his goals was to keep his body under subjection (1 Corinthians 9:27).Certainly this should be the goal for everyone. Self-discipline of our physical, mental, and spiritual qualities are intrinsic to all other successes in our lives. A common quality of most great leaders is self-discipline. We must be able to control ourselves and push ourselves to new and greater heights.

It is always right to push ourselves toward appropriate goals. If we fail to do so, we undoubtedly shortchange ourselves. There is a distinct difference in the accomplishment of those who *make things* happen, and those who *just let things* happen. In my seminars, I have occasionally used a video recording by Dr. Bobbe Sommer titled, "Setting Goals and Achieving Them." Long before that video came to be, Dr. Sommer was asked by a friend to attend a seminar on dynamic leadership. She did not want to go but at her friend's insistence—agreed. During that seminar she became very motivated. She purchased a video recording of that conference. By watching it again and again, she took significant steps toward her new goal of becoming a nationally known motivational speaker.

Nothing in Dr. Sommer's life indicated that becoming a speaker was a realistic goal. She was a homemaker, active in the P.T.A. and very low key in personality. She had never given a speech. She began to take every opportunity to stand before an audience and give a speech, any kind of speech. In the beginning they were mostly five-minute speeches before small audiences.

Even those were scary for her.

Slowly but surely, Bobbie Sommer polished her delivery. She went back to school to continue her education, and over a process of several years, she developed her speaking ability. Opportunities for her grew. Bobbe Sommers is now a popular speaker with engagements all over America and in several foreign countries. Her success began many years ago by setting a specific goal with the determination to reach that goal.

One interesting speaker is Joyce Meyer. She can be seen several times a week on various TV channels and also listened to on many radio stations. She began life as an abused child. At an early age, she married a man who turned out to be an alcoholic and wife abuser. He would move her and her child from state to state often abandoning them in strange locations. Finally, the marriage ended and Joyce was left broke and alone.

Then came a turning point. First, Joyce became a Christian. Her faith grew and her life took on a new meaning. She decided that with God's help, she would begin to speak to people that were hurting and needed encouragement. She began to modestly go out and speak. In the beginning, it was frightening to say the least. Friends discouraged her and critics ridiculed her, but she continued on. Today she is in great demand all over America. It was from her that I heard the story about the teapot. I may not agree with all her doctrine but I applaud her fortitude.

In my early ministry, I pastored a church next door to Colonel Harlan Sanders. The church was just around the corner from the first Kentucky Fried Chicken restaurant. Colonel Sanders had come to Corbin, Kentucky, sixty years old and broke. He started the first restaurant on almost no funds and literally bought the first chickens on credit from Stewarts Grocery—which was next door to his restaurant. The grocery store was owned by one of our church deacons. His house was on the same block as the colonel's, separated only by our church. Colonel Sanders and our deacon, Wilson Stewart, were close friends for the rest of their lives.

While I did not know the colonel well, I did, on several occasions, have conversations with him. He would speak of his goal to build one of the largest restaurant chains in America. Those were pretty lofty goals for someone now in his seventies, virtually uneducated and broke most of his life. Colonel Sanders became a Christian after he was sixty. Once he was amusingly talking about his increasing demand as a public speaker. (He was very distinctive in his southern colonel clothes and white goatee.) He related that he had only attended school for a few years and that when he became born-again he had to give up a third of his vocabulary.

Goals Are Always Important

I recall as clearly as if it were yesterday, when between my junior and senior years of high school, I determined in my heart that I would not settle down into a dull routine. I determined that I would accomplish something with life and see the world. I had no idea at the time that God would call me into the ministry.

While my accomplishments have been minor compared to what many have accomplished, I have had the opportunity to travel to and speak in several foreign countries and speak in some of America's greatest churches. I have often spoken to several thousand people in some of South Korea's largest churches. It is one of the highlights of my ministry.

Set reasonable goals. While many people fail because they fail to set goals, just as many probably fail because they set unrealistic goals. While goals should be challenging they should not be up there somewhere in the stratosphere. Success usually comes the same way that we climb a stairway—one step at a time. When you face and conquer small challenges, God gives you greater ones.

Success is a journey. When I came to Louisiana Baptist University, I told my assistant (now the executive vice president), that we would build the university the same way you push a heavy load over the hill. That we would shove it forward a little at a time, then scotch it so it wouldn't roll back, then shove it again. That is exactly what we did.

We are not to the top yet but we now have students in 48 states and 40 foreign countries. With 1000 domestic students, combined with those studying our courses in foreign countries, we have over 1,300 students. It did not happen overnight. It seldom does. If you check into the background of most overnight successes you will find that they have been working ten or fifteen years getting to that place. But almost always, it began with a goal. In conclusion:

- **Set goals**. You will drift through life if you do not set goals.
- **Set reasonable goals**. Failure to set reasonable goals will bring on frustration, disappointment and ultimately failure.
- **Be persistent**. There is a difference in daydreamers and

goal setters. Daydreamers are always looking for the big strike, to hit the jackpot, or to win the lottery. Goal setters are in it for the long haul.

- **Be unwilling to accept defeat.** If you think it is too late, remember Colonel Sanders. He had tried many things in life with little success. He was well into his sixties when Kentucky Fried Chicken became a success and he became a millionaire.
- **Write down your goals.** Rehearse them in your mind. Speak them out loud. Think about them when you wake in the morning and when you lay down at night.

Remember, success is not wealth or fame. It is not about being a millionaire or having your name in lights. It is first of all, accomplishing all that God has given you the ability to accomplish. After that it is about being happy about finding meaning and contentment in life. Thankfully, contentment and God's will go hand in hand. When we are in God's will, we will be content regardless of what we are doing, even if it never produces what the world calls "success."

"For what is a man profited if he should gain the whole world and lose his own soul?" (Matthew 16:26).

In Summary

I hope that you are enjoying the information I am sharing on the pages of this book. I have tried to give you some common sense answers and encouragement—in order to reach a little higher and dream a little bigger. Nothing is sadder than to see someone who has given up all their dreams and settle into a dull monotonous life.

Remember, God isn't looking for settlers. He is looking for mountain climbers. The higher up the mountain you climb, the steeper the incline. But oh, the exhilaration to reach the peak. Nothing is better than setting high goals according to God's will and then through prayer, perspiration and careful diligence—see those goals fulfilled.

When leaders envision the future, they create a vision that motivates people in the organization and unleashes their power and potential. A shared vision is always the first step toward future success.

Chapter Eleven

Leaders Are Team Builders

For we are leaders together with God.
—1 Corinthians 3:9

One of the most important things you can do as a leader is to surround yourself with a good team. Most of us start out as a one man "team" when the church or organization we lead is small, and we get into the habit of doing everything. In my early years in ministry, my church (which was a start-up) had many needs. I was the janitor, yardman, fire builder in winter, and oh yes, on Sundays—I was the preacher.

As your church or organization grows so must your team grow. Sadly, some leaders never learn this lesson and pretty soon they hit a low ceiling and remain there for life. Their unwillingness to turn loose some things, and turn those things over to others sets limits on what can be accomplished. Even the great Michael Jordan did not win a championship until he surrounded himself with Scottie Pippen and some better teammates. Then the Bulls went on to win six NBA championships.

Labron James, who most would say is the greatest basketball player today, could not win a championship in Cleveland. He went to Miami and won two championships. What made the difference? He was now surrounded by a better team. Building a team (staffing) is not easy. It takes time, requires patience, and there will be mistakes. Even the most accomplished professional will make mistakes and will several times hire or welcome a person onto the team only to find that for various reasons he or she simply does not fit.

When that happens, as the saying goes, "Houston we have a problem." Letting someone go is always problematic. While I will later discuss the firing process, let me tell you upfront, there is not a perfect way. Even the best ways are problematic. That is why great care and much prayer should precede inviting or hiring someone to serve on your team.

Shortly after Sandra Cory and I took charge of Louisiana Baptist University, we felt the need for some part-time office help. We interviewed someone who came to us with what looked like had a very good resume. We found out later that it had been greatly enhanced. Because it was only a part-time position with a low salary we failed to do due diligence and we paid a price for it. I take all the blame; with over twenty-five years of experience I should have been more careful. It became apparent we had to replace her. Sandra was a new administrator and I remember saying to her, "We will do this as kindly as we can, but she will still probably hate us." In most cases it works out that way. Most people will never admit that they were incapable of doing the job and when you let them go in the most diplomatic way possible, in most cases they will still blame you.

In the next few pages I will cover several aspects of assembling a team. The steps are not perfect but they are effective. If a perfect plan exists I haven't discovered it yet. These are methods I have learned the hard way, through trial and error. Believe me, I have had my share of mistakes, but we must strive to create better ways to achieve the best outcome for any given goal.

Over the years, Dr. Cory and I have been able to put together a good team. We have very few turnovers in staff. Several have been with us for approximately ten years and a few have stayed fifteen or more years. They are loyal to us and loyal to the university. Consider the following comments as you put together your staff.

Your staff should not be a clone of you. We all have a tendency to want to hire a staff just like ourselves, others who look, act and think the way we do and have the same strengths. Just the opposite should be true. Interview and find people who bring different strengths to the table; candidates who have great strengths in the areas of your greatest weakness will (yes, we all have weaknesses.) We may not like to admit it out loud, but if we are honest with ourselves we know that we have them and we know what they are.

I remember a conversation I had with Sandra Cory and Dr. George Flannigan. Dr. Flannigan was the president of his own company. He is retired now, but he often taught at both the Pentagon and C.I.A. headquarters. He has a PhD from LBU in Corporate Psychology and is one of the wisest men I have ever met. Early on during our time together at LBU Dr. Flannigan said to me:

> You have the making of a great team. Doc's strength (referring to me) is imagination and vision casting, and Sandra's strengths are organization and management. That gives the team balance, and as long as the two of you will work within the areas of your strengths you will make a great team.

Often when I am delivering leadership lectures, I speak on the need for balance. For example, imagine a drawing of two stick people (kids) on a seesaw. For the seesaw to work properly the two kids need to be about the same size. It doesn't work very well if you have one fat kid and one skinny kid. The fat kid is always on the ground and the skinny kid is always up in the air. You also need balance in your leadership team. You don't need all leaders and you don't need all managers. By the way, Dr. Flannigan's dissertation was on the different mindset between leaders and managers. Leaders and managers have different viewpoints on almost everything. Both sides think theirs is the right view, but the truth is this: Both are important. Each viewpoint should be respected and appreciated.

Having the right people with the right mindset in the right places is essential to team building. A team's dynamic effect changes depending on how the people are placed. John Maxwell in his book, *17 Indisputable Laws of Teamwork*, has this simple list relating to teamwork:

- Wrong person in the wrong place = regression.
- Wrong person in the right place = frustration.
- Right person in the wrong place = confusion.
- Right person in the right place = progression.
- Right people in the right places = multiplications.

Ed Young Jr. in his book, *Creative Leadership*, talks about the hiring process. He states:

> Ask any realtor what the three most important elements in real estate are and you'll hear "Location, location, location." Ask any hiring manager in corporate America what the three most important elements in hiring staff are and you will hear, "Interview, interview, interview."

Our hiring process at LBU involves both myself and my Executive Vice President Sandra Cory. Normally it involves two and sometimes three interviews. On the first interview we both ask questions, and of course begin to form opinions. After that initial interview we compare notes. If we both feel good about the person he or she is invited back for a second interview. Unless Sandra Cory and I both feel good about the candidate, we don't proceed further. Even if the interviewee's resume looks good and all the right answers are given, if we don't feel good about the person we do not make a job offer. (Sometimes it may take a third interview before a final hiring decision can be determined.)

Character is also important in the life of a person who is part of your team. Don't take resumes at face value. Check character references. Forty years ago I made the mistake of hiring a lady that had been fired from a church in a distant state. She had since joined my church. She was sweet, friendly, intelligent and very faithful to our church. I failed to heed the red flag in her past and hired her anyway. Only the grace of God and a lot of apologizing on my part kept our church from a lawsuit. Lesson learned; things are not always as they seem. Check out a person's past history. A call to her previous pastor would have saved me a lot of grief.

Then there is competence. Can the person do the job? Again, checking out a candidate's past work history can tell you a lot. Our university is heavily computerized. It is Dr. Cory's job to find out if the candidate is competent on the programs that we run. Finally, there is chemistry. How will this person fit in with the team that you have assembled? If the chemistry isn't right it really doesn't matter how competent the person is. You often see this with sports teams. From time to time you will see players with obvious talents that are traded from team to team or sometimes given an outright release—because they destroy the positive chemistry of every team that hires them.

Attitude is very important. John Maxwell has said, "Hire for attitude, train for talent." He is pointing out that you can teach people what they don't know, but you can't teach attitude. The most gifted person on the team can destroy that team if he or she has a bad attitude. I tell new members of the team I won't fire them for making mistakes as long as they learn from them. We all make mistakes. I won't fire people for what they don't know. We all go through learning curves. I will fire someone for a bad attitude, which is one thing that will never be tolerated.

Loyalty is important. In fact, it is more than important. Disloyalty is a deal breaker. You have a right to expect and demand loyalty. There has to be loyalty to you, as the leader, as well as the team. Regardless of what other gifts a person possesses, if he or she is disloyal—dismissal is necessary. You need to know that you can trust every team member and they need to know that they can trust you; that you are loyal to them and have their best interests at heart.

Never rebuke team members in public. If you can praise them, then do it publically. If they need correction, then do it privately. One disloyal act by a team member is enough for me to raise a red flag. Occasionally, I have kept on a disloyal team member, offering a second chance which hopefully would result in a redeemed person. A few times this has worked out, but it seldom does. Once a person has shown even one disloyal act, it is nearly impossible to extend trust again.

Cooperation is important. Nothing can destroy a team quicker than someone with his or her own agenda. Remember, you are not looking for superstars, but team members. When people become territorial and fail to work as part of the team they become a liability instead of an asset. That is true even if they have superstar ability. It is essential that every team member must buy into the vision and mission of the institution. If they are just there for a paycheck, they are useless. If that is the case, they need to move on so they can be replaced by others who are fully on board.

A vision statement is imperative, and it must be repeated again and again. It simply cannot be stated too often. The vision statement is the defining purpose of the group and drives the church or organization. Every member of the team must be enthusiastic about where the organization is headed, and understand the role each person hopes to accomplish within the parameters of the group. The future growth and success of the church or organization is dependent upon you, as the leader, and the team members which you have assembled around you.

The Church is not a democracy. (That statement will be perceived as controversial to some.) But show me a chapter and verse in the Bible where the Church has operated as a democracy. Virtually, the only place where I see an election is when the disciples voted to select someone to replace Judas. They elected

Matthias as the twelfth disciple (Acts 1:26). How well did that work out? Matthias goes into obscurity and never plays an important role in anything. Even that election was not conducted by the Church as a whole, only the eleven disciples.

The only other example that we might point to is the selection of deacons. Even in that verse it states, "Then the twelve called together the multitudes of disciples unto them, and said, it is not reason that we should leave the work, and serve tables" (Acts 6:2). Then this group of disciples and elders were instructed to select seven men to be deacons. Again, there is no indication that the congregation as a whole was involved.

Most church models mimic the American democratic form of government where everyone votes and the majority rules. The Church was actually designed as a theocracy. God, through His Holy Spirit uses gifted leaders to lead. It then becomes the job of the leader to inspire and direct the energies of the team of leaders that he has assembled. It is then the job of the leadership team to inspire and direct the energies of that church.

I do not write these somewhat controversial remarks just to stir debate. I write them to emphasize the importance of a loyal, dedicated and visionary team. As a leader, if you want to have a vote taken on everything—then that is your decision. However, churches have split apart on what color carpet should go into the auditorium or what color to paint the fellowship hall.

In Summary

I cannot conclude this chapter without speaking a word about our team at Louisiana Baptist University. Dr. Cory and I have been able to assemble an outstanding team of servant leaders. They are loyal, dedicated and visionary. Each day they make an extraordinary effort to carry out the vision and mission of LBU. I thank God each day for this small dedicated staff and what we have been able to accomplish together.

Chapter Twelve

Leaders Lead by Example

Those things, which ye have both learned, and received, and heard, and seen in me, do and the God of peace shall be with you. —Philippians 4:9

Dr. Albert Mohler in his book, *The Conviction to Lead*, makes this thought-provoking statement, "Leaders are involved in one of the most morally significant callings on earth, and nothing the leader touches is without moral meaning and importance." While the leader shares the same basic moral requirements as everyone else, there are certain virtues that the leader simply cannot do without.

In our Bible verse above, Paul simply says the things that you have seen me do, you should also do. It is not "Do as I say" it is always "Do as I do." Leaders must always set a positive example. Followers should never be asked to follow a certain path until they have first walked the path and shown the way. David Patrick, in a workshop which he titles, "Lead by Example" states, "The question before us not 'will we lead by example?' but will we lead by a positive example or a negative one?"

Effective leaders have a "Do as I do" mentality, not a "Do as I say" way of leading. Nothing will destroy the morale of an organization faster than the, "Do as I say philosophy of leadership. Nothing you say will ever have the same lasting effect as much as the things that you do. St. Francis of Assisi stated, "Preach the gospel at all times, when necessary use words." History is full of both good and bad examples of leadership. On the positive side, there are leaders like George Washington, Thomas Jefferson, and others among our nation's Founding Fathers. We might also mention Abraham Lincoln and Ronald Reagan.

President Lincoln led our nation during one of the most turbulent chapters of this country's history. Reagan became president during a time when our nation suffered from the malaise brought on from the previous administration. Using his leadership skills, personality and great optimism, President Reagan lifted the United States from its doldrums and reinvigorated American pride. He also ended the Cold War. Our most excellent example of leadership is of course, Jesus Christ, our Lord and Savior.

> "So after He had washed their feet, and had taken His garments, and was set down again, He said unto them, know ye what I have done to you? Ye call me Master and Lord: ye say well; for so I am. If I then, your Lord and Master have washed your feet; ye ought to wash one another's feet. For I have given you an example, that ye should do as I have done unto you" (John 12:12-15).

> "For this you were called, because Christ also suffered for us, leaving us a example, that you should follow in His steps" (1 Peter 2:21).

There are also many examples of negative or bad leadership. Three men especially come to mind: Adolf Hitler, Jim Jones and Osama Ben Laden. Great leaders must always set good examples and demonstrate outstanding character. John Maxwell writes, "The bottom line is that the effectiveness of the communication relies more on the character of the messenger than the content of the message." Great leaders must demonstrate humility. Again, quoting Albert Mohler:

> Get this straight; leaders will be humble, or they will be humbled. The virtue of humility is deeply rooted in the Christian's understanding of our human frailty. History is replete with examples of those who have been humbled, but this seems to be one of the hardest lessons for leaders to learn.

An Attitude of Gratitude and Humility Are Essential

Sometimes there is a misunderstanding of the true definition humility. As I mentioned earlier in this book, Paul's statement in Philippians 4:3, "I can do all things through Christ which strengtheneth me" can be misunderstood. Looking at just the first part of that verse it would seem that we are reading the words of a brash braggart, but when we read the entire verse we see that just the opposite is true. We are reading the words of a dedicated humble servant of Christ.

The first step on the road to humility is understanding that *all* good things come from God. If you have unique talents, where did they come from? GOD. If you have great leadership skills, charisma, innate perception and outstanding communication skills—they all came from God. If you have been more successful than those around you, then it is not a time for pride but a time for gratitude and humility.

Great leaders are always willing to admit mistakes. All of us have failures. It is a part of life. The important thing is that we learn from our mistakes, and do our best not to repeat them. The leaders who are strong enough to admit that they are sometimes wrong, demonstrate character and set a good example. Sometimes this can be done by using self-deprecating humor. People are impressed by those who can occasionally laugh at themselves. Rather than diminish the leader in the eyes of his followers, this type of humor actually demonstrates a sense of confidence and comfort.

Former President George W. Bush often used self-deprecating humor, especially when he would bungle or mispronounce words. This is in sharp contrast to the former president, Barack Hussein Obama, who rarely—if ever admits a mistake. For five years everything was blamed on Bush and when the expiration date on that excuse came due, it became the fault of Obama's advisors, the Congress, the media or the Pentagon.

An interesting repartee took place when George Bush was invited back to the White House for the unveiling of his presidential portrait. While tension must have been great, both men handled it well. Obama thanked Bush for leaving a really good TV sports package at the White House. George Bush in turn, when his portrait was unveiled told Obama that in times of decision he could look at the portrait and ask, "What would George do?" Sometimes humor can diffuse difficult situations.

Honesty is central to good leadership. Followers must know that the words of their leader are truthful and that he or she will stand by those words. Nothing will destroy a leader's credibility quicker than evidence that his words cannot be trusted. Remember Obama's words?: "If you like your doctor you can keep your doctor, and if you like your health plan you can keep you plan, period." Turns out none of that was true. Those statements along with some other false statements, and some half-truths caused former President Obama's approval rating to fall to the mid 30s for quite some time.

People want the truth. They want to know that they can trust your words. When you damage or destroy that trust it takes a long time to regain it, if ever. Leaders are always dependable. When I played sports in high school my dad always showed up. I was pretty good at baseball. Even in basketball, when I might only get in the game for three or four minutes, my dad was always there.

I did the same when my son and daughter played sports. I was a busy pastor and could have used that as an excuse, but I never did. I wanted to be there to proudly cheer them on! The leader or dad shows up when it matters—every time.

Albert Mohler writes, "The leader is where he needs to be, always." This is not so much a statement of physical presence as it is an affirmation that the leader is always available, fully in charge and ready to lead. Leaders share the glory. Nothing can be more disheartening to a team than to work hard to make something happen, then see the leader take all the glory. Be generous in your public praise, and as I said before, if something needs correcting—do it in private. Never reprimand a team member in public. Loyalty increases when it is cultivated and applauded. If you are loyal to your team then in virtually all cases, they will be loyal to you.

In Summary

Leaders who set poor examples can cripple or even destroy a church or business. I am aware of a church that was located in a city where I once pastored. It no longer exists—because of poor leadership. This happened in spite of the fact that the church had one of the most beautiful buildings in the city situated in a prime location. This once thriving church had approximately four-hundred people in attendance. But it is now closed, and even the beautiful building has been sold.

I also know of another business that was once very prosperous. Recently, that business declared bankruptcy and closed its doors. This happened not because the market changed or the product they sold was no longer in demand, but because of poor leadership. The original founder/owner retired and the new owner immediately began to systematically pay himself and his family members more than the company could afford. It only took about four years for that thriving business to go bankrupt and close up shop.

> "He that trusteth in his riches shall fall; but the righteous shall flourish as a branch" (Proverbs 11:28).

Chapter Thirteen

Leaders Are Vision Casters

Write the vision, make it plain.
—Habakkuk 2:2

In a previous chapter I briefly mentioned that leaders must be visionaries. Because having a vision is vitally important, I feel that I should include a full chapter on the subject. In this chapter, I will attempt to emphasize that leaders must not only be visionaries but they must be vision casters. It is not only important for the leader to have a vision of what needs to happen in the future, but that he or she is able to motivate team members and necessary others to buy into the vision and keep it alive.

The late Dr. Myles Monroe once stated, "If your vision dies with you, you have failed." As I point out in another chapter, visionaries do not accept things the way they are. Visionaries make things happen. They are focused and determined. In contrast to daydreamers who only dream of big things, visionaries attempt and often achieve great things. John Maxwell thoroughly covers this subject in his excellent book titled, *Putting Your Dreams to the Test.* Visionaries begin to put together a purpose, a plan, the right personnel and the needed financial support required to turn the vision into a reality.

Vision and purpose must come from God. God has an eternal purpose for each of us but many times we are not astute enough to determine that purpose. To again quote the late Dr. Myles Munroe, "The greatest tragedy in life is not death, but a life without purpose." The status quo is never good enough for visionary leaders. They are always seeking new ways to be better at what they do. Christian leaders will first seek out a visionary idea from God. Once they have that idea from God they will seek leadership from the Holy Spirit on how to develop and implement a plan to make the vision a reality.

John Maxwell states that we must lead with vision and purpose, rather than positional power. In several of his books he states that leadership is influence. Positon will give limited influence, but if you fail to influence others that your vision is actually viable—then that influence will quickly fade. Joyce Edwards in her book, *Champions Under Construction* states:

> It is extremely important for a leader to maintain a vertical vision. Great effective leaders must cast a vertical vision from God and not yield to a horizontal or man-made vision. It is essential that leaders keep their eyes focused on God's charge and not allow them to stray from their God-ordained vision. The main role and function of the leader is to maintain the vision that God has given him for the church or organization that he leads.

Leaders Must Be Vision Casters

The visionary must also be a vision caster. It is not enough that you have a vision, but you must impart that vision to others. Very few visionary ideas can be accomplished by one singular person. It takes the help and cooperation of others. It has to be repeated over and over.

Ed Young Jr. in his book, *The Creative Leaders*, gives this helpful insight, "People like being a part of something successful – an organization that has purpose, clear direction and a compelling vision."

People need to know where you are taking them. They will forget the vision if you don't remind them of it over and over again. You cannot communicate the vision of your church too much. It simply isn't possible." People want to know where they are going.

A well-known scene in Lewis Carroll's book, *Alice in Wonderland*, is about her encounter with the Cheshire Cat. This dialogue occurs:

> **Alice:** "Would you tell me, please, which way I ought to go from here?"
> **The Cheshire Cat:** "That depends a good deal on where you want to go."
> **Alice:** "I don't much care where."
> **The Cheshire Cat:** "Then it doesn't much matter which way you go."
> **Alice:** "So long as I get there..."
> **The Cheshire Cat:** "Oh, you are sure to do that, if only you walk long enough."

If we have a purpose and a vision then it matters very much which road we take. Some have said it doesn't matter which religion you follow, all roads lead to eternity with God. We all know that isn't true. Christ said, " I am the way, the truth, and the life: no man cometh unto the Father, but by me" (John 14:6). It would be just as ridiculous to think all roads lead to success. It simply isn't true. Casting a vision often takes a lot of time and patience. It also takes work, a lot of work. Big corporations understand this. They spend millions of dollars developing and advertising their brand or product.

Several years ago I gave a lecture on marketing the Church. I used McDonald's as an illustration. I asked my audience, "How many of you have eaten a McDonald's hamburger?" Of course everyone had. I asked, "How many of you think McDonald's has the world's best hamburger?" Not one person answered, "Yes." Then why does McDonald's have the world largest hamburger chain? Clearly, because of intense marketing of their brand and image. Over and over, thousands of times a day the slogan goes out through the media that says, "I'm loving it!"

Every McDonald's restaurant displays their huge golden arches. Sometimes you can see them from a long distance away on the expressway. The company has successfully convinced people that they are the world's best hamburger fast-food chain. Toddlers begin to clap when they see the golden arches. Ask your teenagers where they want to eat; almost always the answer will be, "McDonald's." How many times have you, as an adult, gone through the drive-thru to pick up a quick order of their mediocre hamburger and fries, all because of the company's vision casting (coupled with their convenient locations and fast service located around the world)?

Warren Bennis states, "Leadership is the ability to translate vision into reality." As leaders, it is important to be visionaries, to peruse those visionary ideas with passion, and to impart them into the hearts and minds of those we lead.

In Summary

An astute leader is not just thinking about today, this week or even this year. He or she is looking forward five or even ten years to envision where their church, school or business will be in the future. This visionary leader must develop a plan and then assemble a team that can also catch that same vision and begin to work together to make it become a reality.

"Where there is no vision the people perish"
(Proverbs 29:18b).

Chapter Fourteen

Leaders Are Purpose Driven

For I am determined not to know anything among you save Jesus Christ, and Him crucified.
—1 Corinthians 2:2

Virtually everyone in the religious realm is familiar with the name Rick Warren. He is the pastor of Saddleback Church, a Southern California mega church. He is also the author of a series of books on purpose, in particular, *The Purpose Driven Church* and *Forty Days of Purpose.*

In the New Testament we are introduced to a purpose-driven preacher who lived two thousand years before Rick Warren. In fact this person wrote a major portion of the New Testament. His name was Paul. If we were to describe him we would probably use many accolades such as, greatest preacher this side of Christ, great missionary, pivotal character in the book of Acts, outstanding writer and many other things. But in Romans 1:1, the apostle Paul introduces himself simply as "Paul, a servant of Christ."

In 1 Corinthians 15:10a, Paul wrote, "But by the grace of God I am what I am." One thing this servant of Christ knew for certain is this: He knew what his purpose was. In 1 Corinthians 2:2, his steadfast dedication to the Lord is clear, "For I determined not to know any thing among you, save Jesus Christ, and him crucified. "

Paul's sole purpose in life was to obey Christ and to spread the message of salvation wherever he went. Satan continually buffeted him, but nothing could stop Paul from fulfilling his purpose. He faced prison, stoning, shipwreck, rejection and finally martyrdom, but nothing could take him away from the purpose he had envisioned.. His epistles are filled with statements about setting goals such as pressing for the mark of the high calling and running to win the race (Philippians 3:14).

Stay True to Your Purpose

Every leader should have a supreme purpose, with an end result in mind. Once that purpose has been established then nothing should push a leader off the road toward that purpose—not people, not obstacles, not circumstances or setbacks. Achieving that purpose will not come easily. You will face obstacles, setbacks, disappointments and desertions. People you counted on will let you down and sometimes allies will become enemies. But if the goal (purpose) is worthwhile you cannot allow those things to stop you. Remember, we are talking about a *purpose* not a *preference.* Preferences can be compromised, suppressed or even abandoned, because the effort is not worth the reward. Preferences are not worth dying for. Purpose is.

At age nineteen, I moved to Ohio and took a job with RCA Whirlpool. I had finished a year and a half of college, but had run out of money and had to drop out. I went to Ohio to hopefully save some money and one day re-enter college. Shortly after joining RCA Whirlpool the company held their annual factory-wide inventory. Because I had completed some college courses my boss put me in charge. The inventory went very well and I received a promotion and a raise. About six months later I was given another promotion in charge of a department.

I was twenty years old and had men my father's age working under me. I was elated. I was on the fast track. I determined in my heart I was going all the way to the top, but God had other plans. He had been working on my heart for several months and during a Wednesday night service at my church I went forward and surrendered to preach. This was in July of 1961. I did not announce a call, I surrendered. There is a difference. In that instant the entire purpose of my life changed. The next day I gave RCA Whirlpool my two week notice. Two weeks later I left for seminary, and a little over three months later I started my first church. (I will discuss that in another chapter.) The point is this: My entire purpose in life changed. It has not changed again since that day, and things have worked out pretty well. I believe that is the way it should be.

Once you have found your purpose, abandon everything else. Invest everything in that purpose. That is especially true if that purpose is ministry. That is what Elisha did. He was out plowing his oxen when God called him. He killed the oxen and burnt the plow and probably had a celebration barbecue. It was his way of announcing that his purpose had changed from plowing to preaching.

I often challenge people to find a meaningful purpose in life. Find a purpose that is higher and nobler than you and then with God's help—set out to achieve it. If you are to be an effective leader, you must first firmly establish in your mind what your purpose is—what your goals are and what you hope to ultimately accomplish. You can never be a strong leader if you do not firmly established your purpose. Otherwise, when opposition comes, when people disappoint you and failures test your resolve, you will abandon that purpose

Look at your purpose as a ship's rudder. Purpose is the rudder that guides us through the storms of life and eventually gets us to our destination. Dr. John Rawlings used to say, "Don't be afraid to try something…anything that you do more than what you are doing now will make you more successful than you are now." I believe that one of the reasons why so many churches are failing today is because they have forgotten their primary purpose. The purpose of every church (led by the pastor) is clearly spelled out in Matthew 29:19-20:

> "Go ye therefore and teach all nations, baptizing them in the name of the Father and of the Son, and of the Holy Ghost: Teaching them to observe all things whatsoever I have commanded yeo: and lo, I am with you always, even until the end of the world."

The Church's purpose is clear and simple. Everything a church does, every action it takes, should be done with one purpose in mind—to win more souls, to baptize those who receive Christ and to disciple them. When churches get back to making the Great Commission their top priority, they will thrive again and grow.

In Summary

I have often conducted workshops connected to my book, *Ten Principles of Success.* I always begin by asking this question, "How do you define success?" For many people success centers on having the biggest house on the block, having the most expensive car on the street or achieving wealth.

While there is certainly nothing wrong with being financially successful, I have met many people with an abundance of material wealth who are dissatisfied with their lives. They discovered that "stuff" and more "stuff" does not bring happiness. I believe that living a life of purpose does.

If you ask the average church to instantly give you a purpose statement, many would stumble for words. Every church should have clearly defined purpose statements that include these points: As a church, why do we exist, what are our goals and how do we plan to execute those plans or goals? The reasons should be explained from the pulpit and discussed frequently among church members.

How can a church effectively move forward if it is not even clear about the purpose for which it exists? That is also true for our own, individual goals and purposes. They must be clearly defined and skillfully pursued with unwavering determination .

Chapter Fifteen

Leaders Are Passionate

For I could wish that myself were accursed from Christ for my brethren, my kinsmen according to the flesh. —Romans 9:3

Paul was certainly a man of great passion. I refer you to the verse above. Here is a man willing to not only sacrifice his body, but also his eternal destiny for his kinsmen. Few would be willing to sacrifice their lives for others, but virtually no one would face eternal damnation for the sake of others. Passion shaped Paul's entire life. When we first meet him in Scripture, he is passionately trying to rid the world of Christianity. He was first a zealot *against* Christ but once converted, he became even more passionate *for* Christ.

In Acts chapter nine, Paul is on his way to Damascus seeking out Christians that he might bring bound to Jerusalem. Once there, they would be tortured and many of them even killed. It is on the road to Damascus where Paul encounters Christ and his life is forever changed. That is what takes place every time someone has a true salvation conversion experience. Paul would never be the same and we should also experience that same change when we receive Christ as Savior. He turned all his passion toward Christ. When we examine all the things that Paul accomplished it is nothing short of extraordinary. Remember that he did this with all odds stacked against him. He was driven by an internal passion and a deep abiding love for the Lord.

Passion is an extraordinary thing. It has been called, "The winner's edge." Much too often, good ideas fail for lack of passion and dumb ideas succeed because of passion. On that pivotal evening in July of 1961 when I surrendered to the ministry, the following day I went to my boss to give him my two weeks' notice. He was amazed. I still remember his surprised reaction. He said, "I thought you liked this job and you have a great future." I agreed that I thought I had a bright future, but not with RCA Whirlpool. When I surrendered to God's calling to the ministry on that July evening, everything changed. Within a few weeks I moved to Sommerset, Kentucky and enrolled in Bible College.

I believe all those decisions were the right moves for my life. When someone surrenders to the ministry they *should* put all their "eggs" into that one basket. I realize that not everyone can act as quickly as I did. I was twenty years old, single and had no debt. It was easy for me to make a life-altering change. Those were the right decisions for me. But then I made a decision that most would say was illogical, unwise or just plain DUMB.

Three months after I entered seminary I decided to start a church. Keep in mind that I had been in the ministry for only about four months. I had very limited speaking experience and had grown up in a small church; one that did not have a Sunday school or any type of a discipleship program. To say I was green is an understatement. I was bright iridescent green. The odds were against me but passion caused me to look past the probability of failure and see the possibilities. I don't remember having a single doubt that I would succeed. Failure was not an option.

I chose a building about ten miles outside the town of London, Kentucky. Originally, it had been a two room dwelling. It had been vacant for several years and was being used by a few chickens as a nesting place. In order to use it, my dad and I installed sheetrock, replaced the broken windows and covered the floor with the cheapest linoleum we could find. Since it was early autumn heading toward the colder months, we also installed a small stove. It turns out we seldom used the stove because the building was normally so packed with people that the body heat kept everyone comfortable.

A nearby church gave us some pews and an old piano that they had in storage. Another supplied a box of well-used song books. You were blessed if you were able to get one of the few books that had both front and back covers. My retired grandfather helped me build my first pulpit out of plywood and we were ready to go. We began with a ten day revival. I prayed that we would have fifty people attend the open service. Around seventy showed up, if I remember correctly. That was more than the building was designed to hold.

The next day I set three poles out front and stretched a large tarp from the front of the building to the poles. I borrowed sixty to seventy chairs from the town's funeral home, and for the remainder of the revival I stood in the doorway and preached to both those inside and outside. Each night the building was packed and many of the borrowed chairs were filled. I only had one message titled, "Jesus Saves."

Each night I would read a different Scripture, give it a different title and basically preach the same sermon, "Jesus Saves." Over a dozen people actually did get saved. I set a date two Sundays later to baptize those folks at a local farm pond. I awakened that Sunday morning and was surprised when I looked out the window. During the night we had experienced an unseasonably early snowstorm. That afternoon after the morning service we had our first baptism on the church grounds, with snow on the ground. (The water was actually warmer than the air.) Shortly thereafter, I organized the church with around forty members. After six months we were averaging approximately sixty people in Sunday School attendance.

I have shared this rather long story simply to show the power of passion. By all odds, my church should have failed. It succeeded for two reasons: First, there was the undeniable power of God; and second, there was a passion that looked beyond the obstacles and saw the opportunities. Passion is a powerful thing. Passion drove Columbus to cross an uncharted ocean to discover a new continent. Passion caused Washington to leave his comfortable home and plantation in Virginia to lead the Continental Army against the British. Surrounded by a group of equally passionate men, he laid everything they had on the line to establish a Constitutional Federal Republic with a representative democracy—one nation under God.

Virtually every great event in history has come about because of passion. Most of us start out to accomplish our goals with great passion. It may be to build a successful company, to serve some great humanitarian cause, or in the case of those of us called of God—to build a great ministry. The problem is that over time, most people will lose much—if not all of their passion.

As president of Louisiana Baptist University, I travel a great deal. It is sad when I visit so many churches where the passion is virtually gone in both the pulpit and the pew.

After over fifty years in the ministry, I understand. Boy, do I understand! There are few jobs as taxing as the ministry. People will disappoint you. You will be lied about and lied to. Not only will your words but even your motives will be tested; there will be people you trust who will turn against you. If you want to quit, I can give you many reasons to quit. I can give you just one reason not to quit: You work for God.

In the third chapter of 1 Corinthians, the apostle Paul wrote that we are co-laborers with Christ. What could be greater than that? If you happen to be someone who is about two quarts low on passion, then now is the time to reclaim the passion that motivated you in the first place. Without great passion you will never be a great leader. I like Paul's farewell message, "I have fought a good fight, I have finished my course, I have kept the faith" (2 Timothy 4:7). Now is the time to renew your calling, replenish your passion and finish strong.

In Summary

We all have events in our lives that we can call defining moments. One of mine came when I was only twenty-one. I had just finished preaching a sermon when I was approached by an elderly preacher who happened to be in the crowd. What he said to me was something like this—Son, I really enjoyed your message. I once preached like that; after a while you will settle down.

Because of the pastor's age and my youth, I did not smart off at him. But when I got to my car I promised God I would *never* "settle down." I didn't want to end-up like that preacher—without any passion. That was fifty-five years ago and I have not settled down or given into mediocrity. I am still very excited about preaching the gospel.

A few years ago I preached to 12,000 people in Seoul, South Korea. The following Sunday I preached to 12 people in Waskom, Texas. I preached the same message with the same passion. You see, the numbers don't matter. Our passion should not be about circumstances or numbers. Our passion should always be about sharing the gospel.

Chapter Sixteen

Leaders Learn to Manage Time

Redeeming the time, because the days are evil.
—Ephesians 5:16

Philosophy

I have attended some time-management workshops that mostly deal with charts, graphs and log books. Many times their goal is to sell you their beautifully printed daily planner guides. They include charts, calendars, sometimes even names of state capitals—plus a daily schedule where you can list your appointments. Some are leather bound and your name can be embossed on the front cover. They can cost up to $150.00. They are nice but not necessary.

My contention is that time management is not so much about carrying around a leather bound book, but it begins with a philosophy. A philosophy that time is valuable and what I do is important, and that I am going to plan my schedule and use my time wisely. How you plan your day and schedule your time is many times the difference between success and failure. You must get the philosophy right or no amount of encouraging books will help you.

My vice president, Dr. Sandra Cory, is probably more qualified to write this chapter than I am. She is perhaps the most organized person I have ever worked with. Over the years I have learned something about timelines. Dr. Cory has developed them into an art form. For example, the biggest event of the year at our university is graduation week.

We have students coming in from several states and even a few foreign countries. We conduct twenty separate workshops, host a Thursday night banquet, a Friday morning breakfast for graduates and alumni, and a Cajun Feast on Friday afternoon for nearly five-hundred people. We spend nearly $14,000 on food for those three events. All of that besides the actual graduation itself, which is sometimes nearly 1,000 attendees, it is a big event.

Graduation is in May, but Sandra begins her timeline in January. It is my job to have the speakers lined-up in December. In January, she begins to design the brochure. In February, it is mailed out to thousands of people. Over the course of two to three months multiple mailings go out. There is also the organizing of three meals, ordering robes, preparing and printing the graduation diplomas and brochures. Additionally, a great number of other details are taken care of right down to making sure there are centerpieces on the banquet tables and fresh flowers on the stage for the graduation. ceremony.

Everything related to graduation is organized on a timeline with certain things to be completed by certain dates. Because of careful well-thought-out organization, our graduations are always spectacular. Time management is tricky, but when done properly it can bring balance to our lives and put us more in control of the circumstances that surround us. Time management also requires a tremendous amount of self-discipline.

Balance

Time management brings balance. Unimportant things do not crowd out important things. Important things move to the head of the line and things get done in their proper order. Proper time management also helps hold down frustration. Have you ever been around people who are always in a hurry, often frustrated and never seem to be caught-up with their work? Perhaps they back track themselves and travel down the same street six times on the same day. Maybe you have met someone who seems to never be in a hurry, is never frustrated and yet at the end of the day—has completed all necessary tasks.

Control

Time management also puts us in control. We should control our events and not let events control us. I understand, that is not easy. Situations can come up that are out of our control. But the person who uses good time management controls his or her schedule better than the person who has no schedule.

Most people live their lives out of control, pulled one way, then another. They are constantly frustrated and non-productive. Many times we are out of control, and our lives are out of control. Hopefully you will complete this chapter determined to be better organized and take control of your life. Remember, we are not talking about being perfect, just better.

Self-Discipline

Time management requires self-discipline. We must discipline ourselves to develop and stick to a schedule. We begin the day with a set of objectives in mind and a plan on how we achieve them. We discipline ourselves to follow a schedule and not get diverted into other things. This is not always easy to do because things always come up. For a pastor, keeping to a schedule is sometimes is simply not possible. People get sick and are in the hospital or there are even some unexpected deaths in the church congregation. Those are things you cannot avoid. There are also many distractions.

Earlier, in Chapter Six I addressed the issue of time wasters. We should always strive for self-discipline in our work habits, our personal habits and even our eating habits. Thirty five years ago a young pastor asked me to preach a revival at his small church in Battle Creek, Michigan. Each day we would visit almost every family in the church. Finally I told him that he was creating a monster.

First of all, visits should be targeted at reaching new people, not just drinking coffee with the members. Second, I asked him what he was going to do when the church grew so big that he could not visit everyone. They are inevitably going to say, "My pastor does not care for me anymore, He used to visit every day and now has not come by for months."

As a pastor, I would tell my people that if I haven't visited your house this year, then count yourself lucky. It means you haven't had a major illness, there have been no deaths, your kids aren't on drugs and your spouse isn't filing for divorce. When pastoring a church we must discipline ourselves or we will run ourselves to death doing unimportant things.

When I was 27 years old I attended a pastor's school in Hammond, Indiana. At that time, First Baptist was the largest church in America. Today, I think it is the twelfth largest. The school was taught by Dr. Jack Hyles. One of his lectures was titled, "Let Your Schedule Become Your Boss." He explained that the average pastor or CEO does not punch a time clock or have a boss. He went on to explain that a pastor should set up a weekly schedule and stick to it. That struck home with me. It makes good sense.

The average person is more reactive than proactive. In other words, we simply react to what comes our way rather than planning, scheduling and controlling the situation. That simple statement had a profound effect on my life.

As a pastor I scheduled prayer time, so I would not be neglectful. I scheduled sermon preparation time, so I was not up at midnight on Saturday night searching through sermons trying to find something to preach. I blocked off two afternoons of 3-4 hours for each visitation. Nothing could be scheduled during those two blocks of time. If you are not diligent with your scheduling, you will find that your week has been filled with unessential things that are self-defeating, and will not build your church.

In Summary

It is impossible for any pastor to have a schedule carved in stone. In any given week, unexpected things happen and they must be dealt with. Once they have been handled, go back to your regular schedule with regular prayer time, regular study time and blocks of time set aside for visitation and soul-winning. Successful people are disciplined people. They control the situation instead of the situation controlling them.

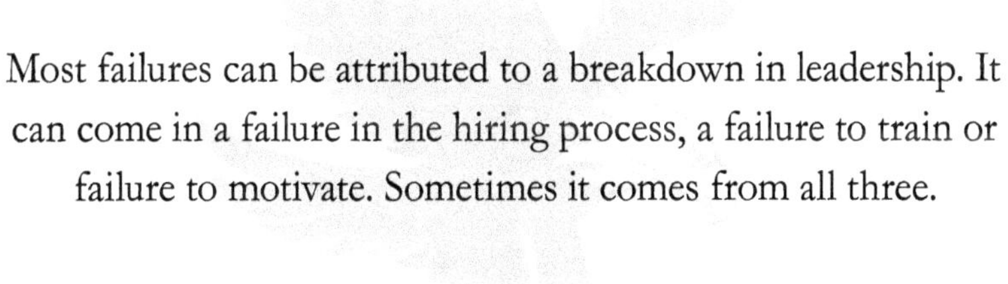

Most failures can be attributed to a breakdown in leadership. It can come in a failure in the hiring process, a failure to train or failure to motivate. Sometimes it comes from all three.

Chapter Seventeen

Leaders Understand the Importance of Prayer

Come unto me, all ye that labour and
are heavy laden, and I will give your rest.
—Matthew 11:28

Prayer should be one of the easiest things we do, but many times it is the most neglected. Prayer is our connection to God. It is our power source. Every year in the fall, I travel to Orion, Michigan to preach a Sunday through Wednesday Bible conference at Shalom Baptist Church. I have been there sixteen times. While I am there, I normally also preach chapel at Midwestern Bible College. Shalom Baptist Church was co-pastored by Dr.'s Harry and David Carr. Dr. Harry Carr recently passed away, he was a great man. They were great hosts, always providing an excellent hotel room and a huge basket of fruit and other goodies.

When I arrived for one of the conferences about six years ago, the church staff explained that there was a special event in town, and that they were simply unable to book a hotel room for me. They asked if I would be willing to spend the first night in one of the dorm rooms at the college, and then hopefully move to me a hotel for the remainder of the meeting. Of course that was fine. The room was clean and comfortable with a private bath and a radio rather than a TV. Being tired from traveling, I decided to retire early and listen to the radio in the dark.

To my disappointment, when I turned on the radio nothing happened. I turned on the bedside light to see if maybe I had neglected to turn something on. Immediately, I saw the problem. The radio's cord was stretched out across the floor, but it was not plugged in. I plugged the cord into the wall outlet and it worked fine. You see, everything needs a power source. You can have the very latest gadget, an expensive laptop or the very best smartphone, but they are all useless without a power source. God is our power source and prayer is our connection to Him.

Dr. Yonggi Cho is pastor of the world's largest church, Yoido Full Gospel Church, Seoul, South Korea. During a question and answer session it is reported that someone asked him, "Dr. Cho, how do you start your day?" The answer was, "I begin each day with four hours of prayer." Someone spoke up asking; "What do you say for four hours?" Dr. Cho's answer was, "Oh I don't talk much, I mostly listen." I have no way of knowing if that story is true or not but I don't doubt it. God's giants are usually great men of prayer.

One cannot talk very long about prayer without mentioning the name George Mueller. He is perhaps the greatest prayer warrior that ever lived. During the mid-1800s, he was director of Ashley Down Orphanage in Bristol, England. During his ministry he cared for over 10,000 orphans. He, during that ministry raised what today would be millions of dollars never asking anyone for help, but simply putting his needs before God through prayer.

There are many interesting stories about George Mueller, but my favorite one centers around one particular breakfast. It seems that one morning when the children came from their rooms into the dining hall they found the table neatly set, but absolutely no food. Mr. Mueller asked each of them to be seated so he could say grace. With heads bowed (I am sure that most peered with one partially open eye) as Mr. Mueller began his customarily prayer. "Lord we thank you for the food we are about to consume."

What food? There was no food. Suddenly there came a knock at the door; Mr. Mueller went to the door and opened it to view a rather frustrated young man. The man explained that he was the driver of a delivery wagon. It seems that a wheel had run off and the wagon was wedged in a ditch. He went on to say that his delivery wagon contained fresh milk and pastries and they would soon spoil in the heat. He said, "Mr. Mueller could you possibly use them?" The wagon was quickly unloaded and the children sat down to a delicious breakfast of fresh milk and pastries.

How many times have we missed a blessing simply because we failed to ask God? The Bible says, "Ask and it shall be given you, seek and ye shall find" (Matthew 7:7a). Dr. Elmer Towns wrote an entire series of books on prayer. They are some of the best I have ever read. Once while speaking at my home church he said that most people pray with their fingers crossed behind their back. They pray with very little faith, that what they are praying for will really happen. Christ said if we have faith the size of a mustard seed we can move mountains. Notice, he did not say pumpkin seeds which are quite large and visible. He said a mustard seed. Have you ever seen a mustard seed? It is a tiny black speck. If you laid it in the palm of your hand it would hardly be visible to the naked eye.

Dr. Elmer Towns in his book, *How to Pray,* suggests that it is good to have a time and place to meet with God. I fully agree. Often early morning is the best time to meet with God. I know that my pastor makes it a practice to rise early so he can have a quiet time with God before his family rises. Anytime and anywhere will work, but I have always seemed closest to God when I could find a quiet place to kneel. When I was still an active pastor I would find time each week to go into our church sanctuary and pray at the altar. Later I developed a habit of going into our sanctuary normally on a Saturday, and stopping at each pew to pray for the people that would occupy that pew on Sunday. Because people are creatures of habit and often sit on the same pew often, I could pray a personal prayer for those people. It was a time that I enjoyed. It only took a few minutes and it always got the preacher (me) ready to preach on Sunday.

I have also had some great prayer meetings while driving on long trips by myself. Sometimes I have had conversations with God that lasted for hours. I say conversations, because that is what it seemed like. And yes, you can pray with your eyes open. Regardless of how you do it or where you do it, always make time for prayer. It is some of the most important time you will ever spend. If you are a leader or aspire to become a leader, it becomes even more vital. It can be the difference-maker in your church, your company or your school. We all need direction and the leadership of the Holy Spirit in our churches, businesses, and families.

In Summary

I believe that morning is the best time to meet with God, but the time and place is not important. The important thing is that you do it. Count it as one of the most important activities of your day. Get excited about meeting with God. Remember the importance of prayer. Daniel prayed even when it put his life in jeopardy. Prayer should be just as important to us. Daily prayer will sustain us as we face the challenges of life.

A leader is someone who facilitates change. It therefore follows that a leader must be flexible enough to cope with changes such as technological advances, shifting demographics and social trends. He or she must be able to determine the difference in long lasting trends and passing fads.

Chapter Eighteen

Leaders Are Consensus Builders

Without counsel purposes are disappointed: but in the multitude of counsellors they are established. —*Proverbs 15:22*

Many times I have heard pastors complain that they had a great idea, but when it was presented to the church it was shot down. Often the problem is that they did not take the time or make the effort to first build consensus. By building consensus, you can move the church to your view point so that when you finally present it, there is a very strong possibility that it will gain approval with very little dissent. I say very little dissent, because it is very difficult to get 100 percent approval on anything. In virtually every congregation there are a handful of people that will always vote "no" on everything. (You are probably thinking about those people right now.)

What do I mean by consensus? For example, an idea comes to mind that you think will improve and benefit the church or organization which you lead. (Hopefully, it came from God.)

You think about it for weeks, you pray about it. You research it to see if it has worked at other places, and you even discuss it with other leaders. Finally you are fully convinced that your idea is a winner, and you present it to your church only to see it voted down. You are crushed, enraged and disgusted at their short-sightedness. But the reason the idea was rejected could be your own fault. You presented something and asked others to grasp and approve of an idea in only five minutes, an idea which you ruminated over for weeks. All this could have been avoided if you had taken the time and made the effort to gain consensus *before* presenting your idea to the deciding group.

How do you gain consensus? First, you arrange several one on one meetings with some of the most influential people in your group or church—people you can trust and people you know have your back. Over coffee you explain in detail what you want to do and why you want to do it. One by one, you begin to build a group of allies who are convinced and buy into your idea. They begin to take ownership of the idea and discuss it with others, as if it were their idea. All this takes time and patience. But when you bring it up months, or even years later, people have already decided this is what they need to do.

When I was 27 I moved to Cincinnati and took on the leadership of a young church that was only three years old. A small 40 x 80 building on a slab had already been built and Sunday School was held in an old house that was on the church's property. We grew rapidly and it soon became apparent that we were going to have to build a larger building. In this situation the need was so great that it did not take long to get consensus. In a matter of months I secured plans, hired a contractor and built a 50 x 100 building with a full basement for classrooms.

Considering I was only 29 and had never built a building before, it is pretty amazing that the church was willing to place that much confidence in me.

The church continued to grow and in a couple of years we were at about 70 percent capacity. The problem that arose was the lack of parking. We only had a small lot with about 25 parking spaces. People were parking as far as three blocks away. We were in a residential neighborhood with houses on equally small lots so buying houses and tearing them down was not a good solution. I began to contemplate moving and building a new church. But how could I ask to do that? We had just built a new building two years before, and now I would ask the church to locate several miles away and build again?

I can only imagine if I had put the idea to a vote at that point, I would have only received two affirmative votes; one from me and one from my wife. She would probably vote "yes" out of loyalty. So I began a long and patient journey to build consensus. I took two years before I felt confident enough to present my relocation plan to the church. There were only about ten negative votes and they came from a few elderly people who walked to church. (They also agreed once I assured them that we would provide a van to bring them to church.) Consensus had worked but it took many one on one meetings, and a clear cut vision on how the expansion and move would occur. By taking time to build consensus, in just two years we had secured one of the most desirable locations in the city and built a beautiful 550 seat auditorium.

I learned something important during those years. Don't pick the fruit until it has had time to ripen. If I had tried to push my idea through without taking time to build consensus, it probably would not have gained the needed votes to move forward. Even if it did pass, the vote would have been much closer to 50/50 and I would have surely lost some families.

When contemplating a substantial move or change, it is important to do the following things: First, make sure it is the right move. Second, make sure you have all the facts, and develop a plan and then take time to build consensus.

In Summary

Timing is everything. Big decisions deserve a lot of prayer and planning and above all, they take time. Patience truly is a virtue. Seeking godly wisdom is an integral part of consensus building. Let the Lord steer your ship and you will arrive at your destination when the time is right.

> "Hear counsel, and receive instruction, that thou mayest be wise in thy latter end" (Proverbs 19:20).

One of the functions of leadership is to define your purpose and objectives. Unless you have a clear picture of what your objectives are, then you are like a blind bowman shooting at a target he cannot see.

Chapter Nineteen

Leaders Are Decision Makers

...but as for me and my house, we will serve the LORD.
—Joshua 24:15b

Let me begin this chapter by saying that there is a difference in being a decision maker and in being a dictator. Dictators operate on the theory of "My way or the highway." They lead through intimidation and seldom listen to advice or entertain opposing opinions. Open discussion is not only frowned upon, but often outright forbidden. Having set the record straight, leaders must be decisive and willing to make difficult decisions.

Earlier I discussed the importance of team building. A wise and good leader will always build a good team around themselves. This team should be comprised of men and women who have shown a love for God, a love for the organization they serve and loyalty toward their leader. They must have also demonstrated wisdom and good godly discernment. Your team members become a valuable asset as you plan and implement programs that will help the church or organization you lead move forward and succeed.

Once there has been open discussion of any given subject it is your responsibility to either alter or approve the final decision. Making that final decision is not the responsibility of the team, the deacon board, the trustees or any committee. As the leader, the responsibility is clearly upon your shoulders. You cannot shirk from that responsibility. Hopefully, there can be unanimity and agreement on the final decision. Every effort should be made to achieve consensus (see my previous chapter on consensus). But ultimately the responsibility is yours. God has placed you in a position of leadership and decision making is part of the job description.

When there is unanimity and agreement then decision making is easy. If there is lack of consensus and agreement, then decision making becomes much more difficult. Some decisions you make will please some people and disappoint or even anger others. But you are required to make them. If the division is deep enough and the action can be delayed, then in certain instances it might be prudent to defer action. Although in some situations decisions cannot be put off. In all cases you must not be seen as weak or unable to come to a decision. Your statement should be something like this:

> I have decided we should delay action until we have had time to further study the situation and come to a better informed decision. At that time it will be decided exactly what action we should take. Lest you think I am too ridged or dictatorial go with me through the process of decision making.

Begin with Prayer

No important decision should be made until you have spent not minutes, but many hours in prayer seeking God's direction.

Gather All Pertinent Data

In order to make an informed and correct decision you must do your homework. Gather all the information that you can. If you know others who have had to deal with similar decisions, then have some conversations with them. See how they arrived at their decision and what the results were.

Seek Consensus

Once you have made a decision on the course of action you plan to take, then invest the time to try to bring your team on board. Involve them in conversation and ask them to contribute their ideas. Hopefully, the end result will be enthusiastic support.

Have an Implementation Plan

Before you announce your decision you should already have a plan of implantation in place. Describe what is needed, and how the plan will be set into motion. Present the positive effect that this action will provide.

Take Small Steps

Drastic change normally will face more stiff resistance. If the plan can be implemented in small increments people are more likely to buy in and agree to it. Most people don't want to budge from their comfort zones. If the change can be more gradual, it has a much better chance of success. Change takes time.

Put the Organization First

Make sure that the things you want to do will benefit the organization that you lead and not you personally. This is not about getting your way or enhancing your resume. The welfare of the church or organization which you lead must always come first. Your thoughts should never be, *How will this help me, but how will it bene it the group or company that I lead.*

Expect Resistance

Expect resistance and never take it personally. The issue is not between you and those you are appealing to. How you approach change is the difference between change and no change, the difference between progress and no progress.

People are by nature resistant to change. I doubt if there is a pastor alive who has not heard the phrase, "Well we have always done it this way" or "We have never done it this way before." As a leader, it is your job to put forth a sound and reasonable explanation why the change should take place. You must also clearly enunciate what your goals are and what reasonable outcomes to expect. You must be prepared to answer opposing questions with kindness, but also with authority.

Be Willing to Take the Heat

Leaders and decision makers almost universally can count on coming under fire. It is part of the job description. Anytime a leader tries to develop people in the pursuit of organizational progress, there will almost always be those in opposition. It is not necessarily you they do not like, but it is your actions that they oppose. While we should always be cautious that our leadership style is not offensive, we must also accept the fact that criticism from others is a part of leadership.

General Colin Powell has stated, "Making people mad is part of being a leader." While no one likes conflict, leaders who are constantly more worried about being popular than being effective will rarely confront people who need confronting. They do not challenge the status quo. Those leaders ultimately end up hurting their own credibility and the effectiveness of their organization.

If you want an example, simply look to the greatest leader ever—Jesus Christ. While artists often portray Jesus standing with hands outstretched and a halo above his head, in reality his ministry was anything but serene. He brought a revolutionary message to the people of His day. He told them to stop believing what they had been taught all their lives and to follow Him. He was loved by some, hated by others.

Jesus was revered and reviled. His life was in constant danger. He called the religious hierarchy whited sepulchers and hypocrites. He turned over the tables of the money changers in the temple. I have often said, "Jesus comforted the distressed and distressed the comforted." And to some extent our ministries should do the same.

I close this chapter with a statement that is not original to me. I read it somewhere, but I am not sure where. The statement is this: "The best decision makers are those who are willing to suffer the most over their decision and still retain their ability to be decisive." I give credit to whoever wrote those words of wisdom.

In Summary

I learned very early on in my ministry that every organization must have a leader. This is especially true of a church. Somebody *will* lead. It may be you, it may be the chairman of the trustees, the head deacon or even the deacon's wife; somebody *will* lead. I decided early on that if somebody must lead, then it probably should be me. This need for leadership also applies to universities like Louisiana Baptist University, a company or a business, and also when it comes to personal and family decisions—someone always leads.

I will add here that nowhere is leadership more needed today than in the American home. Leadership begins at home. If you are the head of the household it is your responsibility to lead. But you should always lead in a loving, Christ-like manner. Christ was willing to die for the Church. As leaders, we should be viewed as decisive—leading with a loving, caring and forgiving spirit. A leader should be the one person who can always be counted on, even in the most trying circumstances.

Chapter Twenty

Good Leaders Finish the Job

I have fought a good fight, I have finished my course, I have kept the faith.
—2 Timothy 4:7

The apostle Paul is one of my favorite writers. That's probably not surprising; he is almost every Christian's favorite writer. So many of my favorite Bible passages come from the pen of Paul. My all-time favorite is Philippines 4:13, "I can do all things through Christ that strengtheneth me." I discovered that verse early on during my first year of ministry. I had just turned 21 and had planted my first church after only a little more than three months in the ministry. As I stated in a previous chapter, to say I was green would be a gigantic understatement. I was bright, glowing, iridescent green.

The longest speech I had ever given was a five minute book report in high school. I determined that if I was going to successfully grow and lead a church I must grow my confidence and leadership abilities. I began a search for books on self-confidence and leadership. Today, if you go to a bookstore you will find an entire section on those subjects, but back then very few books were available.

By the providence of God (and I do believe it was providence and not luck) I came upon Philippines 4:13, "I can do all things through Christ that strengtheneth me." All of a sudden a lightbulb went off in my head. There was the answer. I did not need more self-confidence, I needed more confidence in God. I made it my life verse and for over fifty years when I sign someone's Bible I always add Philippians 4:13.

My second favorite passage from Paul is probably the one printed at the top of this chapter, "I have fought a good fight, I have finished my course, I have kept the faith." Satan could not stop Paul even though he tried. He faced almost everything possible; beatings, stoning, shipwrecks and long periods of time in prison. Yet he was virtually unstoppable. He had but one purpose in life; to serve and glorify Christ

At the time of this writing I am in my 57th year of ministry. I don't know how many years I have left, but I have determined in my heart to finish well. I came along at a time when I got to know several giants in the ministry who were still active in their ministries well past what most would consider retirement age.

I am thinking of men like John R. Rice and Lee Robertson. I also think of my long-time friend Dr. John Rawlings who lived to be 99. Even up to the last few months before he passed away, he still went to the office every day. He would call me almost every week and I always looked forward to those calls.

Two of my longtime hero's and friends are Dr. Robert L. Sumner and Dr. Elmer Towns. Both are well past normal retirement age, but are still very active in the ministry. Dr.

Sumner is in his mid-nineties. He has written approximately fifty books and still continues to write. Two years ago he and I conducted a three day Bible conference for Dr. R. L. Hymers, Jr. in Los Angeles. Dr. Summers is still as powerful as ever. He has a Doctorate of Sacred Theology from LBU.

Dr. Elmer Towns is one of the most exceptional people I have ever met. He was co-founder of Liberty University along with Jerry Falwell. He has written over 120 books and continues to regularly produce new ones. Even in his mid-eighties he continues to travel around the world holding Bible conferences and seminars. In 2007, LBU presented him with an Honorary Doctor of Letters degree.

Great things are never accomplished by small-minded people or people who are quitters. If you plan to lead accept the fact that you are going to face opposition, disappointments and occasional setbacks. Not everything you try will succeed. Count on the fact that there will be some failures along the way. If you check the background of some of America's greatest leaders you will usually find some failures in their past.

I remember walking through the huge building of Landmark Baptist Church with their pastor, Dr. John Rawlings. At the time they were running 4,500 in attendance and were listed in the top ten largest churches in America. I was in my 20s, but I still remember Dr. John saying, "Not everything we try always works. We have had many failures along the way, but we have had enough things that worked to build what you see."

The important thing about failures is not to repeat them. Instead, use them as lessons to keep you from failing in the future. I remember hearing Dr. Rod Mastellar preach a sermon titled, "A Setback Can Be a Setup to Future Success." Learn from your failures and analyze why you failed. Was it a dumb plan to start with? I have had a few of those. Did I overreach? There, I am guilty again. Did I not do enough planning? Did I not invest enough passion and effort in the project? Did I fail to properly communicate my vision? Did I not bring enough people on board and invest enough finances to properly support the project?

Keep in mind that the easy road is usually not the one that leads to success. If it was easy then everyone would be doing it. Only those who refuse to be stopped will ultimately succeed. I once heard Dr. Jerry Falwell make this statement, "You measure people not by what they accomplish, but by what it takes to stop them." Recently during a three hour layover at Dallas Fort Worth Airport, I read a book by Dr. Elmer Towns, in which he recounted some of the difficult early years at Liberty University. The university was just getting off to a good start when the Jim Baker scandal broke. Almost overnight donations virtually dried up.

Even though Liberty University was not involved there was a huge backlash against all television ministries. Many just shut down and it almost destroyed Liberty. Soon the university was a hundred million in debt. In a single day they laid-off thirty percent of their staff. Curriculum was cut back and the entire university was scaled down. The university could have easily gone out of business.

But Dr. Falwell and Dr. Towns were determined not to let that happen. In addition to cutting expenses everywhere they could, they began to seek out new sources of revenue. It was then that Jerry Falwell began to emphasize the Faith Partners program, asking thousands of people to send just ten dollars each month. These monthly gifts of ten dollars each generated enough funds to keep the university afloat. Today, Liberty University is the world's largest Christian university with over one hundred thousand students. What if they had given up and quit? Thank God they did not.

I can tell you that during my life and ministry I have faced many obstacles and road blocks. I think most people have if they have lived a while. Many times failure was turned into success on nothing but simple bulldog tenacity, and unwillingness to give up. In my mid-twenties, I determined that I would build a modest home in which to house my family. It was during the time I had taken on the leadership of a small church in Cincinnati, and moved my family into a cramped basement apartment.

I found a small inexpensive lot, and even though I had never built anything, I decided to build a house. My grandfather was a carpenter and my dad was also a pretty good carpenter. My son can also build almost anything. For some reason those abilities skipped a generation and I have none of those skills.

I was completing my doctorate at a semi-local seminary (fifty miles away), as well as pastoring the church. Each night after dinner I would go work on the house until well past midnight. I had very little money so I had to do as much of the work as possible, myself. One night in particular, I was trying to erect a ceiling joist. I was attempting to hold the joist in place over my head and nail it in place. Time after time I dropped it. Finally, tired, beat up and near the breaking point, I sat down on a paint can and cried. Eventually, those tears turned to prayers and I got up to try again. I soon came up with a plan to hold one end of the eight foot 2x4 in place with a rope, while I nailed the other end. Somewhere after 3 o' clock in the morning I finished and was able to go back to our apartment.

Although I was exhausted, bruised with both hands full of splinters, I was elated in spirit—because I had finished the job. There is something very exciting about having finished the job, to have faced a challenge and won. I found that some of those early challenges toughened me up and prepared me for future challenges. Let me share with you some things that I think will help you finish the job:

Lots of prayer. Earlier in Chapter Seventeen, I pointed out that prayer is our connection to God, so I will not go into added detail except to say you cannot over-estimate the importance of prayer.

Surround yourself with good people. Surround yourself with good people to assist and encourage you. Always associate yourself with positive, uplifting people. (See Chapter Eleven on Team Building.)

Continue to learn and grow. Never stop learning and never stop growing. The problem with many people is complacency. That is, when they reach a certain level of knowledge and ability they settle there. The same thing is true of churches. Have you ever wondered why there are so many churches average 100-125 attendees?

It is because that number of people is just enough to sustain a church. With a congregation of that size, a church can have its own building and support an underpaid full-time pastor. The pastor may start with five people meeting in someone's living room, but because the group is committed to growth, they take action and expand the church ministry.

For a while the church rents facilities, then grows enough to buy or build their own building. Once they have a building, a choir and a pastor, complacency often sets in and with it, a certain self-satisfaction. The same thing happens to individuals; we start out with an ambition to learn and grow. But if we are not careful we grow to a certain sustainable level and settle into a dull routine.

Routine stunts creativity and busyness replaces ambition. As we grow older we tend to put away our goals and ambitions and settle for less than the best. Commit to never stop growing and learning. By continuing to forge forward to accomplish new goals, you will be an inspiration and great role model for others.

Remember your initial goals. Hopefully, early on, you wrote down your aspirations and goals; use that list as a guide. Goals are important. Please go back to Chapter Ten and re-read the information on setting goals. Never stop dreaming. I remember a song I heard many years ago. Some of the words really bothered me and are not supportive of hope and a positive attitude: "When I grow too old to dream."

You are never too old to dream. Keep vision alive! Never settle for less than your full potential. Once you lose vision you will be stuck in a place you may not want to be, and for the rest of your life.

Don't let past failures define your future. When I was in the ninth grade I was asked to be in a school play. (I must have not been very good because I was never asked again.) I remember very little about the play except one of my lines. It was, "If first you don't succeed, try, try again." I have found that to be a pretty good philosophy for life.

I will close the final chapter of this book by sharing my favorite poem. I discovered it when I was a first year college student and taped it to the inside one of my notebooks.

If

By Rudyard Kipling (1865-1938)

If you can keep your head when all about you
Are losing theirs and blaming it on you,
If you can trust yourself when all men doubt you,
But make allowance for their doubting too;

If you can wait and not be tired by waiting,
Or being lied about, don't deal in lies,
Or being hated, don't give way to hating,
And yet don't look too good, nor talk too wise:

If you can dream and not make dreams your master;
If you can think-and not make thoughts your aim;
If you can meet with Triumph and disaster
And treat those two impostors just the same;

If you can bear to hear the truth you've spoken
Twisted by knaves to make a trap for fools,
Or watch the things you gave your life to, broken,
And stoop and build 'em up with worn-out tools:

If you can make one heap of all your winnings
And risk it on one turn of pitch-and-toss,
And lose, and start again at your beginnings
And never breathe a word about your loss:

If you can force your heart and nerve and sinew
To serve your turn long after they are gone,
And so hold on when there is nothing in you
Except the Will which says to them: 'Hold on!'

If you can talk with crowds and keep your virtue,
Or walk with Kings—nor lose the common touch,
If neither foes nor loving friends can hurt you,
If all men count with you, but none too much;

If you can fill the unforgiving minute
With sixty seconds' worth of distance run,
Yours is the Earth and everything that's in it,
And—which is more—you'll be a man, my son!

Bibliography

Bennis, Warren, *Leaders*

Carroll, Lewis, *Alice in Wonderland*

DuBrin, Andrew J., *Leadership*

Edwards, Joyce, *Champions Under Construction*

Flanagan, Dr. George, *Profiles in Leadership*

Hybells, Bill, *Courageous Leadership*

Katzenbach, Jon R., *Wisdom of Teams*

Kouzes, James M., *Leadership Challenge*

Kuhn, Thomas, *Structure of Scientific Revolutions*

Lee, R. G., *The Menance of Mediocrity*

Maxwell, John, *Breakthrough Parenting*

——. *Failing Forward*

——. *Put Your Dreams to the Test*

——. *The Success Journey*

——. *The 17 Laws of Teamwork*

——. *The 360 Degree Leader*

Pentecost, J. Dwight, *Design for Living*

Posner, Barry Z., *Leadership Challenge*

Smith, Adam, *Powers of the Mind*

Smith, Douglas K., *Wisdom of Teams*

Towns, Elmer, *How to Pray*

Warren, Rick, *The Purpose Driven Church*

Williams, Dr. Earl, *Steps One Can Take to Develop a Positive Mental Attitude*

Yung, Jr., Ed, *Creative Church Leadership*